BREAKING THE CYCLE OF ADDICTION

For Adult Children of Alcoholics

Patricia A. O'Gorman, Ph.D.
Philip Oliver-Diaz, M.S.W.

HEALTH COMMUNICATIONS, INC.
Pompano Beach, Florida

Patricia A. O'Gorman, Ph.D.
Philip Oliver-Diaz, M.S.W.
O'Gorman Diaz Inc.
East Chatham, New York

Library of Congress Cataloging-in-Publication Data

O'Gorman, Patricia A.
  Breaking the cycle of addiction.   ·

  Bibliography: p.
  1.Alcoholics — Family relationships. 2. Children of alcoholic parents. 3. Parenting. 4. Alcoholism — Prevention. I. Oliver-Diaz, Philip,
1948-II. Title. [DNLM: 1. Alcoholism — prevention & control —
popular works. 2. Substance Abuse — prevention & control — popular works. WM 270 035b]
HV5132.046   1987   649'.1   86-27137
ISBN 0-932194-37-0

© 1987   Health Communications, Inc.
          1721 Blount Road
          Pompano Beach, Florida 33069

ISBN 0-932194-37-0

Photos by Tom Caravaglia.
Cover design by Reta Kaufman

Preface

How to use
Breaking the Cycle of Addiction:
A Parent's Guide to Raising Healthy Kids

Slowly!

Breaking the Cycle of Addiction is designed to be used slowly so that each new piece of information can be digested, tested and integrated into your bank of parenting skills.

As someone who has been affected by addiction or other traumatic childhood experiences you are probably very aware of wasted time, and as a result you want to accomplish all that you can, and "should" have done, yesterday. You may also be somewhat compulsive and as a result you may compulsively try to use immediately whatever new information you have. In reality, you can't live your life that way. To attempt it is only setting yourself up for failure. It is not possible to relearn new patterns overnight. And you certainly cannot deal with the fears that either keep you from having children, or from being the kind of parent that you would like to be, by trying to "do it all now." So be good to yourself. Go back through the sections a second or third time if you need to. You are not in a race. The important issue is to begin to attempt to change those areas where you need to change, not to master all of parenting at once.

Without Guilt

As someone who has been affected by alcoholism or addiction you have been programmed to feel guilty. Part of your recovery is to affectively fight this. Be loving to yourself and use *Breaking the Cycle* to grow, to learn, but not to "beat up" on yourself for what you either didn't know, or didn't have the resources to do.

As a Reference Book

Breaking the Cycle can be used as a reference book to assist you in understanding how addiction, compulsion or childhood trauma has affected you as a child, a spouse, and most of all as a parent, or parent-to-be. Key research findings are noted in the text, and we also provide you with a list of further readings.

We will also refer you to the ever-growing number of 12-step self-help programs, from Alcoholics Anonymous (A.A.), to Al-Anon, Alateen, Adult Children of Alcoholics (A.C.o.A.), to Overeaters Anonymous (O.A.), Gamblers Anonymous (G.A.), Gamanon, Debtors Anonymous (D.A.), Narcotics Anonymous (N.A.), Cocaine Anonymous (C.A.) and Shoppers Anonymous (S.A.), to name just a few.

As a Guide Book

Breaking the Cycle of Addiction can also be used as a guide to specific parenting issues that confront someone who has been affected by alcoholism and from this can be generalized to understand other addictions. We believe that what we say about the alcoholic and the alcoholic family is equally true for any family affected by compulsive, addictive or traumatizing behavior. We will help to guide you through normal developmental issues that confront all kids and parents.

As a Recovery Tool

Breaking the Cycle of Addiction is about recovery. It is about working to organize your life so that you are no longer consumed by the effects of addiction or childhood trauma.

Our goal is to help speed true "family recovery" by showing you, the parent, or parent-to-be, how to make your family "child-centered" as opposed to alcoholic or addiction centered. For it is only at the point when children begin to feel secure and that their needs are safe and will be understood and met, that children in a family with alcoholism, addiction or other childhood trauma can begin to recover. This recovery can and does occur even in active alcoholic, and substance-abusing homes, in sober homes and in homes where parents are adult children of alcoholism or other trauma, but only when the child's needs are addressed.

As a Change Agent

Breaking the Cycle will also provide you with proven parenting techniques. By carefully and slowly utilizing these techniques you can begin to change how you parent, and be validated for what you have been doing right all along.

Our Goal

Our goal is to assist you in your recovery by sharing with you the benefits of allowing your family to become child-centered and 'child conscious'. By showing you how you can enter the wonderful world of parenting, our hope is that you will allow yourself to participate in this world of giving and receiving.

With love, hugs and wishes for rainbows,

Patricia O'Gorman, Ph.D.

Philip Oliver-Diaz, M.S.W.

Acknowledgments

To Charles Flowers and Marie Stilkind for their guidance in organization and editing; Gary Seidler and Peter Vegso for their confidence in us; Betty LaPorte, Patrick O'Gorman, John Thomas, Ronny Figueroa, John Slotwinski, Roland Moses, Carol Booth, Beth B., Sandy F., Phyllis F., Ellen D., Arlene V., Edward W., Zvi Klopott and Olivia and John Reusing for their honest criticism. To the rest of our family, friends, and patients for teaching us what we needed to learn and to the children from Project Rainbow.

Special Acknowledgments

From: Pat to my "son" Tom for allowing me to experience the joys of being a parent.

From: Phil to my "step-children" John, Bridget, Mary and Laurie and to my brother Mike, sister-in-law Jane and nephew and niece, Joe and Tina, for teaching me the real meaning of family.

Dedication

To our parents, from whose struggles with alcoholism and parenting we have learned. And to our spouses, Sharon and Robert, who supported us through the long nights, endless phone calls and rewrites, and with whom we hope to "break the cycle" in the next generation.

About The Authors

Patricia A. O'Gorman, Ph.D., is a psychologist in private practice and the Director of the Counseling Center for Addictive Families in East Greenbush, New York. She is an international authority on substance-abuse prevention and children of alcoholics and directed Prevention Divisions at the National Council on Alcoholism and The National Institute on Drug Abuse and Alcoholism. She was a founding board member of the National Association for Children of Alcoholics.

Philip Oliver-Diaz, M.S.W., has served as advisor to the Federal Government on Alcoholism, Drug Abuse, Prevention and Cross Cultural Issues. Currently in private practice, he also serves as Director of Substance Abuse Services for Rockland County (New York) Mental Health. A national authority on CoAs, he was founding director of a Pioneer Center for Young Children of Alcoholics and a founding board member for the National Association for Children of Alcoholics.

Together . . . they direct O'Gorman and Diaz, Inc., a consulting firm in East Chatham, New York, specializing in materials and seminars on family life and addiction. They also write a parenting column for CHANGES Magazine.

vii

CONTENTS

Part I: What's Normal and Where Do I Begin? 1

1. For Parents Who Are Adult Children of Alcoholics ... 3
2. A Child's View of Recovery ... 17
3. Parenting and Addiction ... 29
4. Parenting as a Team — Parenting Alone 39

Part II: As They Grow ... 51

5. Preparing for Birth and Parenting the Infant ... 53
6. Parenting the Toddler and Pre-school Child ... 63
7. Parenting the School-age Child ... 73
8. Parenting Adolescents ... 87

Part III: Living Through Addiction ... 105

9. Parenting with an Alcoholic in the House ... 107
10. If YOU Are a Recovering Alcoholic Parent ... 119
11. When to Seek Professional Help ... 135
12. A 12-Step Approach to Parenting ... 141

Appendix I: Terms Used ... 153

References and Further Reading ... 155

Part I

What's Normal and Where Do I Begin?

Chapter 1

For Parents Who Are Adult Children of Alcoholics

"Sometimes I am simply overwhelmed. My father was an alcoholic, my mother was the child of an alcoholic, one grandfather was an alcoholic, both my grandmothers were adult children of alcoholics and my husband is a recovering alcoholic. I go to Al-Anon and Adult Children of Alcoholics meetings, my husband goes to A.A. and needs to go to ACoA meetings and my kids think my husband and I have gone crazy. I worry all the time about Leann who is 15 and Mike who is 10. I worry about the damage Jesse's drinking did to the kids. I worry about the effect my ACoA issues have had on them. All I ever do is worry and watch and wait for them to show the signs of alcoholism; it's like waiting for a bomb to drop. This cannot be the way it was meant to be. There must be another way, I'm just as upset now as I was before and I don't know how to be any other way," says Sarah, age 32.

So What's Normal And Where Do I Begin?

Like many adult children of alcoholics (ACoAs), Sarah is in a cycle of fear and despair. She has no guidelines for parenting. Her childhood was one of chaos, confusion, inconsistency and abuse. Like the character in a poem by the alcoholic poet John Berryman, ACoA parents are obliged to "perform operations of great delicacy in complete darkness." Because their own upbringing has been so crazy and confusing, they have no barometer to gauge their own parenting by and are obliged to parent in the dark.

Impact of Addiction

Letting in the light is not easy for adult children of alcoholics. All Sarah knows how to do is wait and watch, which is what her mother did. Sarah needs to find out what family life is like outside her own alcoholic family and what healthy parenting looks like. She also needs to understand there is no such thing as a normal home.

Adult children of alcoholics often think that normal means perfect and that out there somewhere in the world there exist perfect families (Gravitz, Bowden, 1985). No one does well if judged against perfection. The fantasy that other families are normal and perfect leaves ACoAs like Sarah fearful and alone, wondering how to begin to be a healthy parent. The first step in becoming a healthy parent is to discard the notion of perfect, and allow yourself to become teachable and vulnerable as a person who happens to be a parent.

The second step to healthy parenting for ACoAs is to face the effect growing up in an alcoholic home has had on your own parenting. This is not easy. You may find that you are continuing with your children where your parents left off with you.

Having an alcoholic parent has a direct impact on the way you parent. Many adult children of alcoholics have problems with intimate relationships, seek approval constantly and fear authority figures. Some ACoAs over react to changes they cannot control, and tend to be either super responsible or extremely irresponsible. Often adult children of alcoholics are people who see the world as either black or white and have difficulty having fun. Usually, as a product of their tumultuous childhoods, adult children of alcoholics are terrified of abandonment and will do anything to hold onto a relationship (Woititz, 1983). Any or all of these characteristics will interfere with healthy parenting at times. It is no wonder that adult children of alcoholics often feel lost and frightened when they become parents.

If you grew up in an alcoholic home, you probably did not get the nurturing or support you needed as a child and you may still long for that now. Sometimes adult children of alcoholics feel embittered by their childhood deprivation and will resent the nurturing they give their children, especially if the children don't appear grateful for the attention. Of course, children generally aren't grateful for the attention they receive. They feel that they are supposed to be paid attention to, and they are right. An adult raised in an alcoholic home will often not understand this because no one paid attention to them growing up, or the attention paid was inappropriate.

These are some of the negative effects that growing up in an alcoholic home have on your parenting. Believe it or not, there are also some positive effects from growing up in an alcoholic home. Adult children of alcoholics are resilient people; they are survivors. ACoAs also have a great capacity for nurturing and a willingness to help others. Many adult children of alcoholics show tremendous courage and a will to forge ahead in the face of incredible adversity. Among their number are great world leaders, past and present. Our research has shown that ACoAs are more sensitive than the general population to the people around them (Oliver-Diaz, 1985). As you learn to be a healthy parent, you will need to use these and other assets you have to enhance your skills while you work on dealing with your deficits. You will need to assess the specific ways that growing up in your alcoholic home had on you and face clearly what that means to the way you interact with your children.

Some Basic Rules For Making Meaningful Changes

No one can parent without dealing with the way they were parented. You cannot give love and support to your children without tapping into your own experience of love and support. For adult children of alcoholics this can be very painful. It will take courage and commitment to make meaningful changes in your parenting. To make real change you will have to challenge a basic fear of failure. Take the risk. The rules that follow are guidelines to help you on your way to creating a new cycle of hope and love in your children.

Rule: Children need guidance, not control.

"I can't stand it anymore," groans Leann, "my mother just won't stop worrying about me. I'm fifteen years old and she treats me like I'm a baby. She is constantly hovering over me. It's like I'm under a microscope all the time. She is always looking for problems. It's like I'm not supposed to have problems and if I do, *she's* supposed to solve them. She's always telling me what's good for me. When I complain, she tells me that she never had involved parents and I should be grateful she cares about what's happening in my life. I wouldn't mind if I felt she just wants to help, but it feels more like she wants to live my life for me, or with me. She's always complaining how she was robbed of her childhood because she had to grow up so fast because *her* father was an alcoholic. Well, she's not letting me have *my* childhood because she won't let me grow up."

The Hypervigilant Parent

Adult children of alcoholics are hypervigilant. They constantly scan their environment for possible danger, a coping mechanism learned as a child. This hypervigilance makes ACoAs extemely sensitive to their environment. They are exceptionally good at reading the slightest change in mood or situation based on all kinds of observational skills that the general population doesn't use. Obviously if you are a young child in an alcoholic home, this skill of acute awareness is very useful.

But hypervigilance can become a problem for the ACoA parent. Children need to develop self-reliance. The infant needs to learn that all his or her needs will not always be met. The toddler needs to learn many things through trial and error. The hypervigilant parent interferes with this learning process, by reading the child's needs and immediately responding to them. In some cases the response may not be necessary or helpful for the child. Younger children never learn to accept disappointment if all their needs are always met. They grow up with an unrealistic sense that their needs should and will be met whenever they express them. Another outcome of this type of parenting is the feeling of being smothered that Leann talked about, or a feeling that you are defective in some way because you must be watched all the time.

The Anxious Parent

Many adult children of alcoholics suffer from chronic anxiety. As a result of the trauma faced in childhood, they are subject to nameless fears and project these fears on to their family members, in particular their children. This is why children of ACoAs often describe their families as having many of the same fears, anxieties and behaviors as in an alcholic family. It is a logical result of the message that the ACoA parent sends to the children that they are not safe and that something bad is likely to happen.

"I just didn't realize the impact my worrying had on my children," notes Sarah. "I didn't realize that the way I was expressing concern was undermining Leann's self-confidence. I've grown up being anxious, waiting for the other shoe to drop; and it usually did! My mother would wake me up at night to wait with her until my father got home when he was out on a drunk. She would sit in the kitchen with me making small talk while she wrung her hands. Every few minutes she would get up to check to see that my younger brothers were OK and then keep asking me if I was all right. I used to hate that about her.

"There were always problems with money, when I was a child and my mother was always fearful that we wouldn't have enough to eat. Her worrying made her old before her time. It was very sad. Even now as I think back, I feel how sad it was that she spent most of her time waiting and worrying and very little of her life living. I remember promising myself that I would never live like that but I guess I've not been as successful as I thought. My husband makes enough money and has been sober a long time now, but I still worry. Old habits die hard."

Anxious parents create anxious children. An anxious home is one in which fear dominates. Children need a secure environment in which to thrive. Adult children of alcholics need to learn how to feel safe inside so they can communicate that message to their children. If real recovery from alcoholism is to take place in a family, then the heavy cloud of fear and suspicion which hangs over most ACoAs must be lifted.

It can be done. The ACoA parent needs to learn to separate the past from the present. It is very hard for adult children to admit they are finally safe and that they no longer need to be afraid as they were as children.

"I never realized the baggage from the past that I was putting on my kids," Sarah says. "I was walking around as though I was still living with my alcoholic father. I hovered around Leann like a hawk, just like I used to hover around my younger sister. But then it was necessary. I never knew what my mother or father would do, or who would be visiting, my father's drunken friends or my mother's. I forget that the children have a safe home and that Jesse and I can continue to provide that."

Rule: Validate your child's feelings, encourage them to express their feelings.

"I was taught to deny my emotional reality," says Sarah angrily, "so it is difficult for me to know what I really feel, much less what my children are feeling. I don't know what I am supposed to feel in any situation, so I pretend I don't feel anything or fake what I think might be an appropriate feeling. I'm either a whirlwind of emotion or I feel nothing. I know that I've learned to value my brain above my heart.

"Sometimes my contradictory feelings are confusing. When I'm with the children and really close, I sometimes feel jealous of them for having me as a parent. Isn't that strange?"

One of the most poignant struggles adult children of alcoholics face is the search for their true self or the forgotten child within (Whitfield, 1986; Kritsberg, 1986). After years of self-denial and parental neglect, it is painful for adult children of alcoholics to look back to find the emotional connections lost so long ago. One of the special gifts of being a parent is that our children remind us of the wondrous, open, and vulnerable world that children inhabit. Our children help us remember to keep in touch with those aspects of ourselves. For adult children of alcholics, special issues are raised when you try to connect with the child within.

Jealousy: A Special Issue

Jealousy of one's children is a special issue for adult children of alcoholics. It is hard for many ACoAs to accept the reality of their childhoods. As an adult child you may be faced with the strange and uncomfortable feeling of resentment for being a loving parent. This is very difficult to deal with. Like Sarah, many ACoA parents are caught in a web of fear and confusion when faced simultaneously with the contradictory feelings of love and resentment.

As an ACoA you must learn to separate the feelings you have toward your children from those you have toward your parents. The resentment that may rise up is aimed at your parents, but you unconsciously deflect it toward your children. As you build a secure and nurturing home for your children, the child in you will rage at the recognition of the deprivation he or she suffered. It is important that you understand that the child in you wants to get even when it is faced with pain. It may want to punish your children for its deprivation, rather than allow you to nurture your children.

This does not mean that you shouldn't *feel*. You need to feel your sadness for the sake of yourself as well as your children. You will have to parent the child in you and your children with the same understanding and love. You will need to make sure you do not act out anger against your children that is really meant for your parents. In time your anger will resolve itself and you will move to other stages of recovery. Meanwhile, you will need to learn to live with contradictory feelings and keep nurturing your children in spite of the rage it may make you feel.

Sarah is typical of many ACoAs who as adults had to learn for the first time to deal with feelings locked away since childhood, but who now have to be parents and help their children have healthy and full emotional lives. Sarah needs to learn that one can have mutually contradictory feelings at the same time and that that's OK. Like a good many others, she needs to learn to have her feelings and not to minimize or dismiss them.

Denial of feelings is a chief characteristic of the alcoholic family. It is the breeding ground for denial of alcoholism in the adult. Alcohol does not have to be present to have an alcoholic family system. A system that breeds denial of feeling can be called an alcoholic family.

Working on Yourself is the Beginning

The task of the ACoA parent is to break the cycle of denial. Without work on one's self, the family pattern of denial and minimizing of feelings continues and is passed on from generation to generation. Sarah is attempting to break the cycle and so is Mary. "I was lost at first, I didn't know where to begin." Mary explains how she got help.

"A friend of mine had read a book about adult children of alcoholics and gave it to me. I was flabbergasted. I was happy, confused, angry and sad all at the same time. In short, I was a mess. Jim couldn't help. He was too busy trying to get his A.A. program straight. I found a self-help group for adult children of alcoholics and things immediately got better. I found support and validation in those rooms. For the first time, I was told that I was important, that I mattered and that I had a right to feel and express my feelings. For the first time I was told that my parents were the sick ones, not me. I had to admit I didn't know basic stuff about myself so I also entered therapy to help sort out my childhood and find the missing pieces, so I could parent my kids."

Rule: You need to learn how to play with your children.

"I feel so uptight when I take Andy and his friends to the playground," Mary says. "I really never learned how to relax as a child. In my family you stayed ever-vigilant just in case Dad or Mom had a problem. My father was always drunk and my mother was always sick or upset, so who could have fun? Now when my eight-year-old wants to play, I don't know how. Actually it's very painful for me to watch the other parents laughing and being silly with their kids and there I am unable to let go and wanting to so badly. I just have trouble being spontaneous.

"It's also a problem for Jim. I remember the last time we all went out for a picnic together. It was a mess. Jim and I had planned the day so thoroughly there was no time to have fun. We ended up dragging the kids from fun place to fun place and never staying long enough anywhere to enjoy ourselves. I know now the reason Jim and I were afraid of staying in one place is because we don't know how to just have fun and were unwilling to admit it and let our kids show us how."

Mary is not alone. Many adult children of alcoholics have problems learning how to relax and have fun. ACoA parents may view a family outing as a checklist of tasks to be completed. The over-achieving adult child will often over-program family activities. For adult children of alcoholics, going with the flow and letting things just happen is frightening. Breaking the old pattern of compulsive self-control feels wrong and self-indulgent. Many adult children report that when they are spontaneous and let go of some of their control, they feel as though they have been on a drunk. Their only role model for "letting go" has usually been a drunken parent, thus the association between being spontaneous and being drunk is very strong.

Control is the Central Issue

In order for the adult child of the alcoholic to be able to become a free and spontaneous parent, he or she will have to face the belief that being spontaneous is not like being drunk and therefore bad.

But control is like a drug for adult children of alcoholics. They are often addicted to managing everyone and everything around them. This need to control one's environment is learned behavior for ACoAs. If you grow up in a home where you have no control over your environment, you learn to value control above all else because it is what you need more than anything else. The child of the alcoholic wants to control his parents because they won't control themselves. The child of the alcoholic often grows up watching adults constantly lose control and learns to hate any situation where people do not control themselves. This growth pattern has a direct impact on the adult child's ability to let go and have fun.

Mary and Jim will need to work on helping each other let go. This will often happen first in simply learning how to play in small ways.

It may mean at first that Jim and Mary will need to go out alone with no advance planning. It could mean taking one Friday night together and seeing where the spirit moves them to go. This can be like going on an adventure if it is done with the proper attitude and not seen as a prescription for "dysfunctional behavior."

Let your children help you remember how to play. Take time and play hopscotch or jacks or tea party with your kids. You'll be surprised to find that your own child inside you has been waiting for a chance to get out. The rewards for letting your "injured child" out will be manifold and will provide fun dividends in many areas of your life. Planning less and being more emotionally available to your children will increase your ability to really play with your kids and experience joy in your life.

Rule: Life is not black and white. Adult children of alcoholics need to learn to accept the fact that most situations are in gray areas.

ACoAs do tend to see the world as either black or white (Gravitz, Bowden, 1985). That tendency is one outcome of growing up in an alcoholic home. Mary talks about growing up in her alcoholic home and how she learned to think only in terms of extremes.

"There were no gray areas in our home. My father would fluctuate between telling me I was his special wonderful little girl or telling me I was no good. The same was true of my mother. I would come home from school and, depending on her mood or how my father had acted that day, she would be screaming at me that I was nothing but a lazy good-for-nothing brat or her smart little helper. I learned to expect extremes as a way of life. It's all I know. So of course it's hard for me to break the habit of seeing everything in extremes with my own kids. The sad part is I hated it when my parents pulled that all-good or all-bad stuff because it was frustrating and made me feel crazy. And then I catch myself doing the same thing with Bridget, Bobby or Andy."

Confusion about your own feeling states makes it difficult for you to bring emotional clarity to your children. It is much easier to live in a world of black and white. To see the grays in the world means allowing yourself to feel more anxiety about most things. It means realizing there are no pat answers. It means having to sort things out instead of jumping to conclusions. It means, most of all, accepting that *you* are not all bad or good and that your parents were not all bad or good.

Feedback: A Key For Changing Direction

Checking with healthy friends and getting feedback is especially important for adult children of alcoholic parents. You need to bounce your perceptions of your family members off other people in order to really see how your perceptions may have been colored by your childhood experience of living in an alcoholic home. If you view this process of getting feedback as a learning process, it can be fun. It will help you to see the patterns of perceptions you have about yourself, your spouse, and your children. If you recognize that many of the attitudes you have are tempered by your childhood, you will be able to change direction and create healthy role models for your children. Getting feedback will help you to see that intimacy is not necessarily smothering, that being spontaneous is not the same as being irrational, and the letting down and being relaxed will not bring on depression. Getting feedback will help you to see your children in a more objective light.

It takes time to change old habits. All-or-nothing thinking will not go away overnight and you cannot wish it away. It is a learned behavior that will take time to unlearn. Adult children of alcoholics tend to be hypercritical of themselves — an unfortunate quality that makes you frustrated and give up trying to change. If you approach your behaviors needing change as habits which take *time* to change, you will experience a higher degree of success. Behavioral change is a daily struggle, and you will need patience and perseverance to be successful.

Rule: Children need to have clear limits and need to understand what is acceptable and unacceptable behavior.

Adult children of alcoholics have a difficult time with limit-setting. Often either no limits were set for them as children or limits were arbitrary and imposed with violence. In either case, there was no positive role modeling for self-discipline. Adult children of alcoholics have grown up in a world where the unacceptable was commonplace. If Dad wanted to fall asleep in the garage, he did. If Mom was beaten by Dad on Friday night, it was OK to pretend it never happened on Saturday morning. In fact, hitting, cursing, and acts of humiliation are acceptable in many alcoholic homes. Children of alcoholics grow up without knowing what is appropriate behavior.

A basic task of parents is to teach your child guidelines for operating in the world in an appropriate manner. This means learning what acceptable and unacceptable behavior is and accepting limits on oneself in order to model them for your children. Needless to say, ACoAs will have problems teaching these skills to their children, when they have to learn them for themselves.

"I remember a fight Tim and I had a few years ago, in which we were screaming at one another and got violent," Sarah reflects. "He hit me and I hit him back and we were shouting profanities at one another, just the way my parents had done almost every day of my life. I had become immune to that kind of behavior and thought nothing of fighting that way. Leann was about eight at the time. I went into the kitchen to make a cup of coffee and found her under the kitchen table crying. I realized I was terrorizing her the way I had been terrorized. I realized then that hitting and screaming could no longer be acceptable behavior for me, regardless of the way Tim behaved. It shook me up to see her so terrorized. It brought back all my childhood fears when my own parents fought and how I would pray that they wouldn't kill one another. I realized if Tim and I continued to fight that way Leann would learn to do the same thing, and I swore then that I would break this cycle of hate and violence or die trying.

"From that point on I examined my behavior as a wife and parent from a role-modeling point of view. Eventually Tim also saw what we were doing to ourselves and the kids by making that type of behavior acceptable."

Not all of us get shocked into self-examination the way Sarah did. Sarah understands that as an ACoA she needs to examine her actions to see if she is modeling acceptable or unacceptable behavior. She understands that unless she sets appropriate limits on herself, her children will never accept her setting limits on them. She took responsibility for her parenting task by beginning to screen her own and her husband's behavior.

Spontaneous Age Regression

As they begin to deal with the past, adult children of alcoholics come in touch with many overwhelming and painful memories and emotions. For many, these feelings surface when they enter a 12-step recovery program. Here, often for the first time, they share memories of a childhood which they have repressed for many years. That can be disorienting. Many adult children of alcoholics report feeling like emotional volcanoes that may erupt at any time. Indeed an explosion of feelings often surges up during the first years of recovery.

As an adult child, once you begin to come to terms with your past, powerful feelings can be provoked, and you may experience something called *spontaneous age regression*. This is a state in which the ACoA is thrown back into memories from the past triggered by a reminder from childhood, like a particular piece of music or a special phrase someone uses which reminds you of your parents (Gravitz, Bowden, 1985) so you begin responding as though you were six again.

For all these reasons, early recovery is a very difficult time for adult children of alcoholics. In an attempt to explain what is happening to their children or as a way of attempting to find nurturance, ACoAs may reach out in inappropriate ways to their children. They may start to lean on their children for emotional support in ways that breed anger and resentment.

Leann, Sarah's 15-year-old daughter, feels confused and angry at her mother's reaction to Sarah's adult children of alcoholics self-help group meetings.

"I don't understand her," Leann sighs. "Sometimes I think Mom's losing it. She comes home from those ACoA meetings or her therapy sessions either a wreck or on a high. I never know what to expect any more. She gives me all this literature to read and tells me that I have all these problems she has because I'm the child of an alcoholic. She tells me she is going through a tough time because she is having a lot of feelings about her parents.

"She told me about how my grandfather beat her and sometimes touched me in the wrong way. I mean, wow, that totally blew me away! She said she's not sure she's ever felt loved. She even told me once that being the adult child of an alcoholic has affected her sex life and that she was promiscuous when she was younger and now she's afraid of sex, then she asked me if I ever felt that way. Can you believe that! I was totally embarrassed!

"My younger brother Mike found her in her room crying. She was holding a picture of her mother. He came to me totally freaked out. I wonder if she is losing it totally. I'm frightened for my brother who gets upset when Mom starts crying or throwing things. I don't need Alateen. I need to go to a group for children of recovering adult children of alcoholics."

Leann resents her mother needing her support. She wants her mother to be there for her. She *needs* her mother to be a parent. Sarah, on the other hand, is going through a very powerful time in her life and needs to experience what she is feeling. These situations are not mutually exclusive. Sarah needs to find ways to experience her repressed feelings without frightening her children. Often this can be done by learning to share appropriately. Sarah needs to lean more on her husband and program friends and less on her children.

Children are not small adults. They do not need to be sheltered entirely from their parents' emotions, but those emotions should be shared appropriately. Sarah's children are frightened for her and for themselves. Children need a safe and secure environment. When a parent seems emotionally unstable or does things which seem strange, children become insecure and worry about their parents. This creates the same type of stress and tension that exists in actively alcoholic homes.

Reliving Trauma Is Not Necessarily Healthy

Sarah is reliving a traumatic part of her past. She needs to learn how to deal with that experience in a healthy way. Many adult children of alcoholics think that more feeling is necessarily better and that if they keep reliving the traumatic experiences from their childhood, they will somehow exorcise their feelings about them. This is not so. Reliving trauma may turn into recreating trauma which is harmful, and not productive for ACoAs — or, as we have just heard, for those around them. In fact, staying stuck in the past does not allow the ACoA to make the necessary changes in the present. Sharing your childhood traumas carelessly with your children can traumatize them.

Leann was very upset with the information her mother gave her about her grandparents. Sarah needs to examine her motives for sharing that information. If her intention wasn't aimed at helping Leann, then she shouldn't have shared it with her daughter. If it was aimed at getting even with her parents, then she has only succeeded in breeding another generation of resentment in her children.

Sharing Information Appropriately

You must exercise caution and discretion when sharing your childhood with your children. This is especially true when sharing your negative feelings toward their grandparents. Your children should not be put in the position where they must choose between you and their grandparents. This puts your children in the position of choosing between people they love. It is a no-win situation for the children and puts them under unnecessary stress.

Guidelines For Recovery

It is important to share your health with your family. As an adult child from an alcoholic family you are a survivor with many strengths. You need to identify with these strengths and work on the weaknesses. All too often we hear ACoAs refer to themselves as "dysfunctional" because they have identified some negative coping patterns in themselves or recognized an area of life in which they feel blocked. This does not make one a dysfunctional person. What it points out is that adult children of alcoholics, like other people who have come from troubled families, need to examine and change some dysfunctional attitudes, beliefs and behaviors.

Adult children of alcoholics tend to describe themselves in negative terms such as "sick" or "controlling." Who wants a sick parent and what useful purpose is served by describing yourself that way? Does it enhance self-esteem to call oneself dysfunctional? In your family this approach may only serve to increase the level of anxiety and confusion in your children and increase their sense of insecurity.

Children believe their parents. If you tell your young children you are sick, they will believe you. If you tell them alcoholism is a family disease, they will believe that, too. They will not understand it, but they will get the important part of the message which is there is something wrong with them. Children need their parents to help create supportive home environments which give them messages that they are all right. This is especially true for children who have lived with active alcoholism. Calling yourself and your family sick only confuses your children. It is better to understand your character traits and work to change them so that your family sees the product of your 12-step program in you.

Summary

The important thing to remember as a recovering adult child of an alcoholic who is a parent is that you only need to do the best you can in one day. There is no such thing as a perfect parent as there are no perfect children. As an ACoA, you will need to accept that there are certain weaknesses you may have as a parent. But you also have many strengths which you can pass on to your children. You will need to exercise caution in sharing your childhood with your children and in sharing the traumatic feelings you may be reliving.

Recovery is a journey, by turns exciting, disturbing, overwhelming, enlightening, and eventually liberating. The promise of recovery comes from the example of those in the 12-step programs who have learned to live full and loving lives free from addiction and destructive dependencies. The best example of your recovery for your family is to be a consistent parent who can supply a loving and secure environment for his children. Life is a learning process for both parent and child. For adult children of alcoholics there is a great deal to learn. But if you let yourself find joy in the journey, your life and your children's lives will be enriched immeasurably, and each of you can become all you were meant to be!

Chapter 2

A Child's View of Recovery

"I don't care if I get in trouble. I'd do it again. Nobody cares about me. I'm invisible," says 10-year-old Mike, the son of Jesse, a recovering alcoholic, and Sarah, the adult daughter of two alcoholics.

Negotiating Recovery

Mike was caught stealing by Ms. Lewis, the school social worker. He had taken something from another student's desk. Mike was questioned by Ms. Lewis, who knew about Mike's father and had helped Mike when his father was actively drinking.

"I couldn't believe it," Ms. Lewis painfully admitted, "There was Mike in trouble for stealing again. I understood why Mike got into trouble when his father was drinking. I spent many an hour counseling Mike during his father's drinking. But I thought everything would be fine now that his father was sober. Now after talking to him I'm not so sure any more. I've never spoken to such a confused little boy before.

"He told me with his eyes full of tears that he lost his best friend when his dad got sober. When I asked him who that was, he said, breaking out in tears, 'You! You don't care about me anymore!' I realized that once his father had become sober, I had withdrawn from Mike, and that the only way for him to get my attention back was to get into trouble again. I realize now that he was very ambivalent about his father and that he still needed help from me to negotiate his father's sobriety, just like we had negotiated his drunkenness. I realized that in some ways this little boy was more isolated now that his parents were in recovery programs than he was before they went for help. He was mourning many things, including our relationship."

It is not easy for children of alcoholics to negotiate their parents' recovery. It can be a very confusing time, especially for young children. Children need help to make sense of all the changes that take place in a family that is recovering from alcoholism. Change is scary, especially to children from chaotic homes. There are many things you need to consider as a parent in order to help your children negotiate your family's recovery from addiction.

"I couldn't believe that Mike was stealing when his teacher called to let me know," Sarah acknowledges. "He had always been a responsible child and a great help to me when Jesse was drinking. It was hard to believe that now that Jesse is sober Mike would be caught stealing. It wasn't until I spoke to the school social worker that I understood how confused Mike was and how much help he needed to adjust to the changes in our family. Once Jesse and I understood what he needed, we were able to help, and Mike calmed down."

One of the things that Sarah and Jesse did to help Mike was to tell him what was happening to his family. They helped the boy sort out the many things that were upsetting him.

Things That Frighten or Confuse

Hospitals are scary places for children. If a parent was hospitalized, your children would need to understand what happened in the hospital. Children often have very negative fantasies about hospitals, and need to be reassured that their parents are OK. This is particulary true for children of alcoholic parents. Often the parent returning from an alcoholism treatment program will act and seem very different to the children. And indeed if the treatment was successful, the parent has changed in some very importarc ways. This "new" parent will often be confusing to your child. The children need to have the hospitalization explained in a manner appropriate to their ages.

Children may also be confused when a parent joins a self-help group like Alcoholics Anonymous. Children need help understanding where their parents go at night and why. There is a period of adjustment to the newly sober parent which can be extremely difficult for children. Children have all kinds of unanswered questions during the early stages of recovery from alcoholism and they need guidance. They also have very mixed feelings about their family changing. They may feel jealous of a new closeness between Mom and Dad. They may decide that Dad was better drunk if, when newly sober, he takes a more active role in setting limits on them.

Finally, children need to find out where they fit in this newly reconstructed family. They need you as a parent to help them negotiate this very difficult time. Little Mike lost his best friend when his dad got sober because his best friend thought she wasn't needed any more. Often parents make the same mistake. They believe that they are not needed as much because the drinking has stopped. They do not realize that in many ways they are needed more, not less. As parents you need to realize that early recovery is a time of change and confusion for your whole family. Even positive change creates anxiety in your children, and they will need your support.

The Chemical Is Not The Issue

"I wish my father could realize he is an alcoholic and go for help!" laments Maria, a 16-year-old in a children of alcoholics group. "Why?" asks Leann a 15-year-old in the same group. "My father stopped drinking and went to A.A., but he's no better."

From the child's point of view, parental drinking is not the issue. For Mike's sister Leann, getting better means a lot more than not drinking.

"It wasn't always bad for me and my brother Mike when Dad drank," says Leann. "Sometimes Dad was real nice when he drank, and bought us gifts and things. I'm glad Dad stopped drinking because now we have more money, and I don't find him passed out anymore. But many things are still the same. Dad and Mom still fight a lot. They both embarrass me and I'm still invisible to both of them. They haven't learned how to be parents — I still have the job!"

Leann is angry that her parents haven't changed much, even though her father is now sober. For Leann, getting better means changing other behavior besides drinking. Both her parents are adult children of alcoholics and had no role models themselves for healthy parenting. In many ways the problems that Leann faces with them have more to do with the way her parents were parented than the fact that her father is an alcoholic.

Leann's parents need to tune into Leann's needs as an adolescent and her feelings as the child of an alcoholic. Children of alcoholics often feel unloved and responsible for their parents' problems (Black, 1981). They need to feel that they are listened to and that their opinions count.

They need to feel that they are important to you, and that you will be available to them when they need you.

This is a tall order, but it can be done. Studies show that *families can recover from alcoholism* in a relatively short time (Moos, 1984). One day at a time you can develop the trust and closeness you and your children need in order to create a whole and healthy family. The first step is to understand how your children see you and your recovery, to listen to your children with an open heart.

Is That All There Is? Life After Survival

When sobriety comes, the children expect everything to become smooth and wonderful. They are not prepared for the long period of adjustment that Mom and Dad have to go through. They are not prepared for a worsening of the relationship between their parents, which is a common occurrence in newly recovering couples who may be honestly looking at their commitment to one another for the first time in years.

One of the biggest disappointments children of alcoholics face is the realization that when the drinking stops, their lives don't immediately become the fantasy happy household that they imagined. For the children of alcoholics who had ideas of fun and hugs, real life after sobriety can be a shock and a disappointment. This can get played out by the child becoming involved in alcohol abuse or truant behavior.

"I guess I thought that Mom would be like the mothers on TV when Dad got sober," says Bridget, 16-year-old daughter of an alcoholic. "Instead what I got was what I already had but worse because now I couldn't convince myself it could be different. I guess when I think about it, I must have imagined that some wicked witch put a curse on my family and when Dad got sober, the curse would be lifted. Mom would become a beautiful queen, Dad would be the handsome king and I would be the indulged princess. But obviously it hasn't worked out that way."

Loss: A Special Issue

One of the many losses children experience in recovery is the loss of the special role they may have played when their parent was actively drinking (Wegscheider, 1981). Laurie, 13, talks about how she felt when her mother started taking over again:

"I felt very resentful, it used to be just Dad and me, and while I wanted Mom to be part of that, I really didn't have to worry about her butting in because she was drunk all the time or Dad was mad at her. Now I understand, but then I felt really betrayed by Dad when he started to let Mom order me around again. I mean, I used to make sure Dad had supper when he came home from work, not Mom, so why should she get my privileges now? It was very confusing for me. I wasn't used to having Mom as a mother. I was used to treating her like a younger sister and to treating Dad sort of like a husband sometimes and father sometimes.

"I know it was wrong and Dad tells me it wasn't supposed to be that way and that we all need to go back to what we were supposed to be, but I miss being special to Dad. I also don't see where Mom gets the right to boss me around now. I mean she tells me to be home by nine o'clock! I used to stay out to one in the morning whenever I wanted to. So long as I had breakfast ready and went to school and did my chores, Dad didn't care. I feel lost now and angry and guilty for feeling angry. I mean, I should be happy so how come I'm not? Can you tell me why?"

This issue of loss of a special place in the newly sober parent's life is very significant for children of alcoholics. Parents need to help their children adjust to new roles. Parents need to be sensitive to feelings of resentment previously unsupervised children might feel by appropriate parental concern. You will need to allow your child to go through the natural grieving process that accompanies loss. This may include a phase in which your child will try to bargain to retain some of his or her special privileges or tasks.

Laurie wasn't so sure she wanted her mother to make breakfast and take care of her father, especially if it meant that she would lose some of her well-earned freedoms in the process. Laurie's mother needs to be sensitive to the issue and *gradually* take back her role as mother. She needs to inform Laurie that while she is no longer needed to do the mother role in the house, she is still valued and respected. Laurie's mother will also have to examine what a reasonable curfew for Laurie is, given Laurie's past history in the family as a responsible family member.

There may also be a period of anger. Anger is a natural reaction to change and loss. You may be confused by your children's anger at a time when you feel they should be happy. You will need to remember that your recovery from alcoholism or its effects, while it may be something your children want, may still spark fear or resentment.

Eventually children will accept the changes in you, in their families and in themselves, and they will learn to live within a healthy family, but it will take time!

Recovery Is Often Not About Kids

Children are often the forgotten people in the early stages of recovery from alcoholism. Often the first message they get from their parents and the treatment professional is that recovery will not include them.

Leann recalls her introduction to what recovery was going to be like for her and her younger brother Mike. "I couldn't believe it," she said as tears welled up in her eyes. "The alcoholism counselor who was working with my Dad called me and Mike into his office and told us that *we* needed to help Dad, now that he was trying to get sober. He told us Mom and Dad were going through a hard time and that we should try not to put any unnecessary stress on them. On *them!* Can you believe that? What did he think had been going on for the last 15 years? For as long as I can remember I have been trying to avoid putting stress on them. Who did he think was taking care of Mom every time she fell apart? Who did he think did the cooking, washing, Christmas shopping, and counseling for everyone? Who did he think helped raise Mike? And he had the nerve to tell Mike that he was supposed to help Dad and Mom now! Mike was eight at the time and he was supposed to help Dad and Mom? I think all adults are crazy. When do *we* get taken care of? I had to take care of them when he drank and she fell apart, and now I was supposed to take care of them when he's sober? And you know what, I left the counselor's office feeling guilty for not wanting to help out any more! Even thinking about that now I feel angry and like no one will ever see what I need ever . . . ever . . . *ever.*"

Leann's introduction to the helping professions is not unusual for children of alcoholics. Leann was the highest functioning member of her family and the therapist made a classic error. He was asking her to continue raising her parents. He gave her the message that recovery was not going to be about the kids. Parents often fall into the trap of letting the child who became Mother's little helper or Daddy's little girl continue in the role of Superkid after the drinking has stopped. This is particularly true of the sober spouse who has got used to having an extra set of hands around to do the shopping, cleaning, cooking, banking, etc. Leann's parents were concerned that she was failing two of her subjects when they brought her into therapy. It took them a while to realize that Leann was failing because she felt ignored by them and abused by all the adult work she was still being asked to do. Anger in children often gets acted out in behavior such as drunkenness or promiscuity or poor school performance. It is a response to the message that the only way to get taken care of is to be dysfunctional. Children of alcoholics learn early in life that being responsible gets rewarded by more unwanted responsibility (Black, 1981).

You can help your children by letting them know that recovery is a family process. You can help them by giving them an age-appropriate role in the family and helping them to learn how to be children instead of little adults. You can help them by letting them know that your family values each individual equally and that everyone, including the children, will share in the family's attention.

Moving Beyond The Past — Leaving Alcoholism Behind

At all times, but especially during the early recovery stages, it is important to begin to unburden your children from the baggage of the past. In the actively alcoholic family, the alcoholic is constantly focused on drinking. The spouse or the adult child of the alcoholic is constantly focused on the alcoholic. During the time the alcoholic was active, everyone was concerned with parent's drinking. Children expect that to change once a parent gets sober. They expect and really need their families to leave the alcoholism behind. Instead what generally happens in recovering alcoholic families is a demand for everyone to be concerned with a parent's sobriety. This is compounded by the fact that the sober spouse of the alcoholic and the alcoholic may discover that they are adult children of alcoholics during the course of family treatment. All this can be extremely disappointing to the child.

"Most of the time they still only think of themselves. All Dad ever talks about is alcoholism and staying straight, it makes me nuts. It makes me want to go out and get high and get even," growls Bobby, 14. Bobby is the child of Jim, a recovering alcoholic and cocaine user in A.A., and Mary, his wife, who attends Al-Anon meetings. "We still have to make them feel better. They still fight all the time and now they get on my case more than before, because now they think they have to be super parents. Mom is constantly telling me I'm at risk to be an alcoholic like Dad and my grandfather and Uncle Jack. I mean, how does she know I'm going to be an alcoholic? Dad wants me to go to an A.A. meeting with him. I hate alcoholism. I don't want anything to do with it. I don't care if Mom is the adult child of an alcoholic, all I want is a normal family. So what if my Dad doesn't drink or snort coke anymore. He still thinks he's God, and he treats me like a kid. I mean, who does he think did all his work all these years, the tooth fairy?"

'I Don't Care If I'm At Risk'

From your children's point of view when a parent stops drinking, the last thing they want to hear about is addiction. It is normal for traumatized children to want to distance themselves from the source of their trauma once the trauma is over. For children of alcoholics, this often takes the form of not wanting to talk about or hear about drinking or drugging for a while. Your enthusiasm for the recovery programs of A.A., N.A., Al-Anon or ACoA, is not generally shared by the children because it is viewed as a continuation of the family's focus on alcoholism.

A primary fear of parents who have been affected by alcoholism is that their children will become alcoholic. The statistics bear out the fact that children of alcoholics are four times more likely to become alcoholics than the general population (Goodwin, 1973) and are more likely to marry an alcoholic (Nici, 1979; James, Goldman, 1971). This does not mean however that your child will become an alcoholic or drug addict. Your child is at risk for addiction. You can accept that fact just like you accept the fact that your child is at risk for many other diseases that may run in your family, like heart disease or diabetes. You need to educate your children so they can understand what may happen in the future, and then you need to let go. To project negatively about your children's future will create an atmosphere of fear and anxiety in your household which is not good for you or your children. The least affective way to influence your children is by moralizing and smothering them with concern. Let your children know they are at risk when drinking becomes an option for them, but do it in an unemotional way, stating facts and not feelings.

'Help! My Parents Have Freaked Out'

Children need help to understand the 12-step program. Many children whose parents are in "the program" think their parents have entered a strange cult.

Leann explains what life was like after the treatment center when Dad and Mom joined 12-step programs: "It was like they had totally freaked out. My Dad and Mom started talking about the 12-steps of A.A. and God and a bunch of weird stuff like that. I could never get a straight answer from them. If I asked a question about some problem, they would quote some A.A. or Al-Anon slogan or 'step' to me; it was like their brains were controlled by A.A. and they couldn't think for themselves. And my father was always talking about Bill Wilson (the founder of A.A.) and the program of Alcoholics Anonymous. The 'program' — it sounded like they were Moonies or something. I didn't recognize these people at all. At least before I knew what to expect from them. Now it was like they were strangers.

"I mean, talk about weird! My Dad never believed in God and he never went to church. All of a sudden he was talking about his higher power, meaning God, all the time. He made us all say the serenity prayer before dinner. Mom constantly had all these weird women around talking about stuff I didn't understand. I mean, I would listen to them sometimes and all they would talk about was how to live with an alcoholic, like nothing else existed. Sometimes I would see someone crying and talking about how she was the adult child of an alcoholic. Then my mother would get all choked up and look at me like I was going to die or something. It scared me to see those adults freaking out.

"I mean, I thought when Dad stopped drinking, I wouldn't have to hear about alcoholism ever again and now that's all they ever talk about. In a way it's worse than before. Before we never talked about it and we needed to because Dad had a problem. Now he *always* talks about his alcoholism and Mom's also talking about how her father's drinking affected her. I didn't even know he was an alcoholic. I just wish for once we could be a normal family and not be *sooo* heavy!"

Most children are ambivalent about their parents' entry into 12-step programs. Children are usually not informed about the nature of A.A. and Al-Anon and have a great deal of confusion about what goes on in these programs. Since it is natural for them to not want to talk about alcoholism and to put the bad memories of the drinking days behind them, they are confused by their parents' constant focus on the disease. They feel resentful because meetings now take both parents away from them and they see this as unfair. They thought that once their parent got

sober, they would all be together and instead they find there will be less
time together, not more, and on top of that the sober spouse who used
to be home is now also abandoning them.

'I Might as Well Become One, Too' — Feeling Replaced

One often unconscious reaction children have to A.A. and Al-Anon
is to feel that they will be left out of the family unless *they* become
alcoholic or marry an alcoholic. This is a somewhat subtle reaction to
parents in recovery programs. Listen to what Bridget, 16, has to say
about her parents:

"It's like the only thing they care about is the people in A.A. and
Al-Anon. I brought home my report card last week and had straight A's.
I went into the living room to show Dad and he was talking to Mom
about this teenager he met in A.A. who was sober and had been strung
out on cocaine. He was saying how much courage it took for this kid
and how much he respected him. He said the kid asked him to be his
sponsor and Dad said he would. He said that he was going to take him
to a meeting next Friday . . . he didn't even remember that Friday night
was my induction into my school honor society.

"And Mom's no different. All she ever talks about are these young
girls who have real struggles with their husbands and that I shouldn't
complain about my life! I mean, I guess you don't count in my family
unless you're a drunk or married to one. Dad never has any time for
me, but he has for a drug addict. I guess I should become a drug addict
and ask him to be my sponsor; maybe then he'd pay attention to me."

Bridget's parents were totally unaware of their daughter's feelings.
They did not know that she felt undervalued by them. They were not
aware of the messages they were unwittingly sending to her about their
priorities. Certainly, Bridget's father had no idea how replaced his
daughter felt by his decision to sponsor a young person. Parents in
12-step programs need to be tuned into these subtle, powerful, reactions.

The remedy is to take the time to find out how your children feel
about your activity in A.A., N.A., Al-Anon or ACoA meetings. You
need to become sensitive to the feelings of jealousy and competition
that your new relationships might engender in your children. This does
not mean that your participation in self-help programs is bad for your
children. It means that you must respect their reactions and reassure

them that they, your children, are important to you. It means you need to be careful about the extent to which you impose the philosophy of the self-help programs on your children.

What children need most is to see parents who are changing their behaviors to create better communication and greater acceptance of individual differences in the family system. What they need least is to be introduced to an alien set of values and an alien jargon at a very confusing point in their lives. Your enthusiasm for A.A. and Al-Anon would be best expressed by working the principles of the 12-step programs to create a positive, loving environment in your home. This is true family recovery

Stress . . . Stress . . . and More Stress

The most destructive element in an alcoholic family is chronic stress. Stress can cause physical diseases in children such as peptic ulcers, bronchial asthma, high blood pressure, migraine headaches, and backaches. Dr. Timmen Cermak asserts that adult children of alcoholics may be suffering from a variety of post-traumatic stress disorders similar to that noted in returning combat veterans, which is induced by the chronic stress suffered in childhood from living in an alcoholic family system. For some, home is like a war. Stress in an alcoholic home can stem from the controlling behavior of the adult child of an alcoholic or the chronically inconsistent behavior of an alcoholic parent. It is aggravated by the twin fears of violence and the fear that the family will be separated. If incest and child abuse are involved, the stresses are magnified a hundredfold.

All the changes and uncertainty that come when a parent recovers from alcoholism heightens (at least for a while) the stress that your children have to deal with. It is important to help your children develop positive coping strategies to handle the stress in their lives. From their point of view many of the aspects of recovery that you count as pluses, they score as minuses. The new friends, recovery programs, and growth that will work for you will not answer your children's problems.

You will need to help develop a support system for your children. This may include Al-Ateen groups if your children are willing to go. You will also need to create this support system within your family. This can be done by organizing family support meetings each week.

Although anger is a normal emotional response to stress and loss, children in general will feel guilty if they show anger (Youngs, 1985). You will need to give your children the message that it is OK to express anger, to help your children learn how to express and communicate what they feel. This will be difficult if you are learning this skill for yourself at the same time. Just remember, no one grows up having all these skills, and all parents, even those without alcoholism in their families, have problems expressing feeling and communicating with their children. You are certainly not alone.

Guidelines For Recovery

You can break the cycle of dysfunctional parenting. It takes a commitment to listen to your children with your heart and with your head. To succeed you will need to take a compassionate view of the impact your recovery has on your children, and to suspend your own ideas about your children and what they need. To become a good parent you must become teachable, and allow your children to be one source of your education.

This means learning to listen to your children in a special way. Children often speak in codes that need deciphering. Learning to read your child's code and understand his or her feelings will increase the intimacy between you. Letting your child know that he or she has been truly heard and responded to will increase self-esteem in your child and create new possibilities for health and happiness.

Summary

Children need help in negotiating their parents' recovery. Many things about their parents' recovery may be confusing. The self-help programs need to be explained with care and in an age-appropriate manner. You need to ensure that the child is not lost in the confusion of entering treatment and recovery programs. Loss is a special issue for children from alcoholic families. They may act out anger or other feelings as a response to the loss of special roles they had in the family. They will react to any change in the family system. Being available to your children and sensitive to their needs and feelings will make for an easier transition into recovery for them.

Chapter 3

Parenting and Addiction

"I was taught that one couldn't be successful and have a relationship, because relationships took too much work. I certainly have managed to prove that true. I'm not even married and I'm 35. But I am successful. I work hard, maybe even too hard but I'm vice president of a bank. You'd think I'd feel great, (after all, my mother never even graduated from high school) but I don't. I feel empty and scared. I want to be a mother, but I know I'll be a failure," laments Betsy, the adult child of an alcoholic.

Parenting as a Family Tradition

Contrary to what you may have grown up to believe, you *learn* to be a parent. You are not born this way. You learn how to express your love, to give, to ask, to receive. You also learn to negotiate, and to share. Your initial source of knowledge about life is your family. Within your family every new generation teaches the next its beliefs and its rules.

Sometimes these relatively simple sounding lessons of life are difficult to master. The source of this difficulty for the tens of millions affected by alcoholism are their family rules, dysfunctional rules, unwittingly taught from one generation to the next, and unconsciously obeyed.

Often these family rules are unfortunately not perceived as dysfunctional or as having painful consequences. One reason for this is that once we have the conscious knowledge of painful consequences, we feel compelled to change. And change can be frightening. To protect family members family rules are seen as the unique, special way that "this family" relates to the world. To be part of your family, you do as they do. You learn the rules of your family and by learning and practicing what your family holds to be true, you make your family beliefs come true.

Betsy confirms this. "How can I learn to be a parent when I've never even learned to be a child?" she wonders.

How You Learn

Knowing what your family's rules are and understanding how they affect your desire and ability to be a parent is important. But first you need to understand how family rules are taught.

Watching

You first learn by watching. Your parents, grandparents, aunts and uncles model appropriate behavior within your family. They demonstrate how people in your family act. Before you ever speak a word you are taking in the world around you. Some of this you may even remember — memories so early that they do not have words to go with them. These are called screen memories. They may be of being in a crib, throwing food or playing. Or they may be of sensations around us which we record as fear or pleasure.

Listening

Watching is enhanced when you learn to speak. Now you can watch and listen. You have words to describe what you have experienced. Your ability to understand the world has doubled. In homes with alcoholism listening unfortunately can teach that the person who is right is the person who yells the loudest or the longest.

Imitating

You also learn by doing, by imitating what you see around you. Not only do you learn how to perform tasks in this way, but also how to express your feelings as you may have seen a parent do. You may have learned that if you are angry, it's OK to hit your mother as you have seen your father hit your mother, even though you may have been *told* not to hit in anger.

Understanding *how* we learn can help us understand *why* we learned our family rules. For example, Betsy tells us that her father was always late for dinner. "My Mom would yell or cry, but he'd be late anyway. Later I realized that it was because he would stop at the bar. But I grew up thinking that what my Mom felt wasn't important to my father. Dad would ask me how I felt, but I decided that I wasn't very important to him. Look how he treated my mother. I didn't trust him, so I wouldn't tell him what was going on within me. Sometimes he'd cry. Then I would feel sorry for him. But I never trusted what he said, so I never asked him why he was sad."

The rule Betsy learned was "Do not trust what men say." She first learned this indirectly by watching how her father treated her mother.

"I later learned it directly by choosing someone to fall in love with who was just like my father. He'd say all the right things, but couldn't back them up with action. "I'll meet you at six for a drink," he'd offer. Two hours later would come a call that he just got out of a meeting, but he would sound drunk. And when I'd be annoyed, he'd blow up and yell about how unsupportive I was. He even wanted to marry me. I felt that I couldn't put my kids through what I had been through. So I broke it off."

The Development of Compulsive Dependency

One of the most prominent effects of parents with addictions and compulsions is in the tendency of children reared in these families to learn to be compulsively dependent.

Compulsive Dependency — Is a type of *"learned helplessness"* that is unconsciously taught to children from birth. Here the child is systematically made dependent on something or someone beyond themselves. Individual needs are fulfilled through something or someone else and not directly. This leads to a lack of independent action, as the person or the activity on which the dependency is centered becomes the focus of the majority of the individual's emotional energy and time, in lieu of directly taking care of him or herself. Compulsive dependency results in not only increasing the likelihood that someone with the genetic predisposition to develop alcoholism or addiction, will begin to drink, or to use drugs, but also leads to other types of compulsive dependent behaviors such as those noted in adult children of alcoholics. These behaviors include the tendencies to:

— develop crippling dependent relationships,

— compulsively overeat,
— compulsively work,
— compulsively find relief from tension, but not joy in sex,
— compulsively gamble, and
— compulsively shop.

A Reaction to the Need to Master

The infant's first need is to master its environment. A child's first success in mastery is to cry to relieve hunger pains. Children learn that by crying they can relieve their distress. By learning how to relieve their distress they begin to influence, and eventually master, their environment.

The need for mastery over the environment is a life task. At different points in a child's development this mastery will be demonstrated in a variety of ways, from the striving for good school grades to the development of a fierce competitive spirit as seen at high school and college sports' events, to the thrill of stealing and not getting caught.

Dependency is learned as a result of living in a family where a behavior is rewarded one time and punished the next. Children learn to be dependent on cues from their environment in order to know how to act. They are often not taught to follow their feelings but rather to follow the actions of another — to *react* as opposed to act (Mussen, Conger, Kagan, 1969).

In addicted families there is no such thing as learning what is the right behavior as this keeps changing. The perceptive child grows to learn how to watch the family so that under each changing set of circumstances — the alcoholic parent being drunk, hung-over or dry —the child will know how to act. When the cues keep changing and the consequences for mistakes are severe, the child becomes dependent on these external cues in order to know what to do (O'Gorman, 1975). The brighter the child, the more in tune with his environment he will be and the more anxious he will become. Children will know that they are not behaving as they should, and they will be more confused until they learn the alcoholic family rule of not depending on themselves, but rather on the the cues around them.

By learning to trust only external cues, children learn not only dependency, but also learn that feeling good can only come from a source outside of themselves. This helps to explain why many children of alcoholics learn to depend on others and not themselves in a relationship. This is also why many children from addictive families learn to eat, shop, drink, drug, work, gamble, spend, or have sex compulsively.

As Betsy said in a therapy session, "It's taken me a long time to realize that my compulsive overworking and binge shopping filled a false need to be satisfied from the outside. Now when I think back, I can see all the ways my parents gave me things to be dependent on rather than people. I can see that they felt inadequate to meet my emotional needs so they tried to satisfy them with material things.

"I'm not angry with them anymore because I realize it wasn't intentional on their part. I'm just glad that I have learned to become an independent person, able to take care of myself, in a real and direct manner, so I can create new and healthy family traditions with my own children when I have them."

How Addictions Affect Parenting

The authors, relying on their clinical findings and those of their colleagues, find each addiction and compulsion involves the repetition of an action or the use of a substance which once brought enjoyment, and now brings none. Compulsive and addicted people eat, work, drink, drug, shop and gamble for they hope they will regain the earlier enjoyment of these activities. Instead they only find themselves sinking deeper into despair and cutting themselves off from those around them.

We further found that the impact of addictions and compulsions on families to be similar, regardless of the reasons for the development of the addiction or compulsion. When dysfunctional rules are modeled by parents, the family will more often than not, tend to organize around a 'substance' or 'act', instead of organizing around people and feelings.

This creates an environment which perpetuates and breeds addictions and compulsions in the rest of the family membership. It is important to 'break the cycle' and find ways for all family members to be more independent, autonomous choice-makers. To accomplish this parents need to learn to be more nurturing and understanding to the child within themselves and more nurturing and understanding to their children.

There are many addictions and compulsions, all of which affect parenting. These include alcoholism, cocaine and other drug addictions, eating disorders, compulsively working, compulsively shopping, compulsively having sexual intercourse but not enjoying the experience, and compulsively gambling. Each of these again teaches the child rules of family membership, rules which later translate into rules for living. Let's look at some of these addictions and compulsions to begin to understand *how* and *why* the child learns its rules.

Alcoholism

The alcoholic family operates in two different cycles, the *wet cycle*, when the parent/spouse is drinking, and the *dry cycle* when the alcoholic parent or spouse is dry (Bowen, 1971). To understand how alcoholism affects your family you need to distinguish the differences in the way *your* family functions when the alcoholic was/is drinking, and when he or she is not.

In the typical alcoholic family when the alcoholic is drinking, there is more interaction, more contact and more eye contact. This may be mostly negative. The interaction may be yelling, and contact may be physical hitting. Yet there are many secondary gains attached to this. Studies have shown that it is more painful to live alienated from those around you (Bowen, 1974). This perpetuates the cycle of abuse in the alcoholic family. As difficult, or downright bloody, as the contact may be, the family maintains the rules that allow it; for not having contact is even more painful as in the dry cycle.

The dry cycle has been described as like walking on eggshells without breaking any. Or as the feeling you have when you are running out of air but are afraid to gasp. The dry cycle is noted by the absence of contact. It is characterized by withdrawal, for any contact, any comment, any gesture is feared will precipitate another drinking episode. The guilt and fear associated with this is enough to drive family members away from each other. They may stop talking and spend less time together. No one wants to be responsible for the alcoholic drinking. As a result family members are also driven away from their own feelings as they withdraw and repress them in order to protect themselves and their family's temporary peace.

In essence by living with alcoholism you have learned two sets of rules: Rules for the wet cycle when contact was allowed, but more often than not was negative and painful. And rules for the dry cycle when contact was not allowed and was even punished by guilt and total responsibility for what occurred. This led to learning to depend on outside cues in order to determine how to act. These rules and family dynamics teach the child to be dependent.

Eating Disorders —
Binging, Anorexia and Bulimia

There are three types of eating disorders. They range from compulsive over-eating, to anorexia, self-starvation, and bulimia, eating great quantities of food — binging, and forcing oneself to throw up —purging.

While medical scientific experts disagree as to whether one can place an eating disorder as an addiction or a compulsion, Judy Hollis says 'Fat is a family affair' (1985).

Children with a parent with an eating disorder often learn that people are not to be depended upon for nurture, rather they learn to find *comfort in food*, either in its consumption or avoidance. They learn to deal with anxiety, frustration and stress through compulsive over-eating, self-starvation or binging and purging.

Here children fail to learn how to recognize their own needs. Instead the child learns to see food as a way of being *in control* of their needs, and as a way to protect themself from being hurt. This may be learned indirectly by watching a parent, or it may be learned directly by parents encouraging the child to do as they do. Many children of compulsive over-eaters report that the only time they ever felt close to their family was then their parents invited the family to join them in binging. As adults this same behavior is reported as having been learned so well that it is continually being repeated. For example, many report having binged on dates in order to feel safe and close.

Compulsive Gambling

Compulsive gambling is increasingly being seen as following the course of other addictions. Gamblers show dependence on gambling, tolerance, meaning that they need to gamble for increasingly larger amounts of money and to gamble more frequently. And finally when they cease gambling, they experience withdrawal symptoms of disturbed mood or unusual behavior. Many compulsive gamblers are also 'cross-addicted' to alcohol or drugs (Blaszcynski, 1986).

They have in short, the same symptoms commonly associated with alcoholism and cocaine and other drug addictions. Like alcohol use, but unlike cocaine and drug use, not all people who gamble, will gamble compulsively. What makes a difference between those who will socially gamble and those who will compulsively gamble has been traced to four factors:

1. A possible genetic or physical brain defect.
2. Early exposure within a family or peers.
3. Initial large wins.
4. Availability of gambling outlets and experiences (Blaszcynski 1985).

... The Big Win

Families are deeply affected by compulsive gambling, but initially family members may not see that there is a problem. Many gamblers have a great capacity for self-delusion, believing that the next bail-out will send them to "fat city", or the next bet will bring the big win. Many also have great energy and are 'on', hyper, all the time, making them stimulating and entertaining to be around. As a result many families see gambling as the gambler does, as a positive, exciting experience. A spouse may be excited by the possibility of large wins, special trips and the illusion of wealth and power. This may account for the high amount of intact marriages found with compulsive gamblers. Children may find going with a parent to a racetrack exciting and special, even though a parent is not home, and cannot be depended to be present emotionally for a child, for there may be 'Christmas' once a week (Holden, 1986).

... No Longer Unbeatable

A second phase that the gambler goes through comes when they begin to sustain losses. They may begin to be less generous with their money, some even keep a separate 'gambling bank account.' They begin to hoard, and possibly steal money from home or work, so that they can go on with their addiction, much like the alcoholic does with alcohol. Some families will be aware that something is wrong, but they may all hope and pray for a return of 'lady luck'.

... The Loss of Specialness

It is often only when there begins to be less and less money available for the home, a growing fear as to how money will be paid back, and possible threats to life, limb and family members that the family's denial will be challenged. The gambler is now obviously desperate and in the third phase of addiction. Until this occurs many families may enjoy a highly stimulating 'good life' where 'fortune smiles on them' and 'they are special'.

These illusions are very painful to give up. A child loses not only his 'specialness' and the 'specialness of his family', but now is also confronted with depressed and angry parents who will need to be cared for. While their home may not have been 'child-centered' initially, now they may move even further from the possibility that it could ever become child-centered.

Children will often experience a need to rescue one or both parents or to escape. In rescuing, the child may become the family caretaker, and begin to parent the parent. A child born during this third phase may be programmed from birth to deny feelings, and to be the caretaker. Parents who are in this third phase feel abandoned by 'fortune' and are often depressed, having little to give to their children.

In escaping many may cling out of loyalty to the 'family tradition' and may even begin to gamble, to rescue the family financially.

Knowing Your Personal Rules

As parents, it is important to know your personal rules. Much of what you will be reading about in the next two sections will help you clarify these rules. Knowing your rules is important so you can:

Forgive yourself . . . for whatever you have done unknowingly, unwittingly to your children, your spouse, your parents and to yourself. It's not easy but vital in order to live a happier, guilt-free life and hence to become a good parent.

Forgive your parents . . . which may be even harder. However, with knowledge can come ownership of previously repressed feelings, leading to understanding, empathy and eventual forgiveness. It is important to remember that your parents were not malicious. No parent wants a child to grow up sick or unhappy. If a parent who has been affected by alcoholism can be faulted for anything, it is for being too loyal to what *their* parents have taught them.

Change . . . is possible, but only after you know what you need to change, why you developed it to begin with and when you have learned new coping tools to replace the old ones.

Knowing your personal rules allows you to decide which ones you may want to change, and which ones to keep. Knowing yourself also allows you to accept yourself as a recovering person, and as a parent or a potential parent.

Summary

Parenting is a learned skill. Rules are learned from one's family, and when alcoholism has been part of the family system, these rules are often dysfunctional. Learning what your personal rules are can help you to understand why they were developed and to change the ones which interfere with your parenting.

Chapter 4

Parenting as a Team — Parenting Alone

"I used to wonder why we ever got married. We argued before we married, and argued even more after. When the kids came, our arguments turned into major campaigns against each other. We both felt trapped, especially me, just like my dad was. How could I leave Diane with an infant and a two-year-old? I felt I should have left before we had kids. But here I was. I felt responsible for there being no affection in my home. I withdrew from Diane, just like Dad did from Mother. Diane, on the other hand, just wanted me to go. She felt that we just couldn't make a go of it," says Matthew, 30, the adult child of an alcoholic, married to Diane, 28, also an adult child of an alcoholic and a child incest victim.

Power Struggles

Power struggles are part of many relationships. To have a power struggle does not always mean to be caught in one. Couples may go through periods of greater or lesser emphasis on power issues.

How do you know you're in a power struggle? Power struggles occur when two people attempt to impose their personal view of the world on the other. If only one of you is right, or can be right, then you are in a power struggle.

The Impact of Addiction

When alcoholism is added to family dynamics, power struggles are almost certain. Power struggles emerge in two major ways. One way is as a reaction to change. Part of recovery is change. Many of those in recovery from alcoholism, or in recovery from the effects of living with someone with this disease, become caught in power struggles with a loved one, as they change the rules of the relationship. Change is difficult, particularly if only one member of the couple is recovering, and so it is resisted (Wilson, Orford, 1978). Alternately, some couples in recovery begin to have enough distance from the dynamics of their relationship to allow them to see their relationship more clearly, less emotionally, and to realize that they have been involved in power struggles all along (Steinglass, 1980).

How Power Struggles Develop
... Family Traditions and Crises

These power struggles stem in part from the crisis-orientation found in families with alcoholism. Families with alcoholism rock along from crisis to crisis. These crises are often triggered by power struggles within the family, that is, one family member wanting another to behave in a certain way, and not accepting an alternative behavior or viewpoint.

Matthew provides an example: "I remember my first intellectual battle with my father. He was drunk and asked me what I was studying. I told him mammals. He then quizzed me on what makes an animal a mammal, and he was wrong. I even showed him in my textbook what was said, but he said that they were wrong, and I was stupid for believing them. So we battled over whether the textbook and my teacher were correct. He just couldn't accept any other point of view but his own. Looking back on it, these battles were the only time my Dad and I would speak."

When a crisis occurs in a family with alcoholism, it is almost as if the fire alarm has sounded and each person mans his or her battle station. In a crisis each person's role is more clearly defined, and each person can predict how the others in the family will act, for each part has been rehearsed many times before. In a crisis when one looks below the surface behavior, there is more order and communication in the family than when the family is not in crisis. In these non-crisis times, there is isolation and even alienation between family members. Contact and emotional closeness, even if it is negative, is the emotional gain that keeps the family generating crises, so that they will communicate and have some predictability in their lives. In this way family members affected by alcoholism and other addictions sustain a series of traumas. Around these crises the family organizes and behaves in a predictable, almost prescribed, but painful manner (Bowen, 1974).

... Developing a Personal World View of Cause and Effect

In the closed family system, the family's unique set of rules function as a protective shield around the family. It protects the family's special traditions, such as always naming the first baby girl after the mother, or always eating pork on Christmas Eve, and negative traditions such as father's coming home drunk on Friday night and waking up the family. As such, a family system gives the family's world predictability, even in crises.

As a child grows up, he or she learns how to be a member of the family. He learns the family rules, that is to see the world, and to love and be loved, only as taught by his family. This is in part due to the isolation that the family lives in, isolation which effectively limits the exposure of the child to experiences outside the family (Wolin, Bennet, Noonan, 1979).

Family rules and rituals are very important in defining how a family is unique. The more closed the family is, the more each member will adhere to the rules. Closed families, such as those affected by alcoholism, cling to their special ways of making sense of the world, their rituals, their rules, for not to do so would invite change, and disruption. Change in a closed system is always to be guarded against as it threatens the way things "should be". Change is frightening, and results in increased anxiety, and for a system already loaded with anxiety, any addition is felt to be too much (Papp, 1983). This rigidity itself may become a family rule.

In a closed system other points of view are stubbornly kept out. This wall of isolation means that little can change within the family as this protects them from dealing with the anxiety and fear that change would bring. As a result, family members in a closed system develop a highly personal way of making sense of the world. This allows them to feel that there is cause and effect which they can influence, and which is predictable, even if it is painful. Predictable pain is often easier to bear than unpredictable change.

This personalized family system of cause and effect, and the personalized expression of love, are spawned by a need to reduce the amount of anxiety which is common in closed families. This personalized system also has many secondary gains, not the least of which is the perception of personal control, *if* one follows the family rules (Wolin, Bennet, Noonan, 1979).

... and Compulsive Dependency

In order to maintain an illusion of control, dependent people will cling to their family's viewpoint of cause and effect. As a result they begin to develop an increasing reliance on their family's way of doing and seeing things, as opposed to developing their own ways. Unconsciously, they begin to derive much of their own personal identity from the way they have accepted their family's approach to the world. The more they cling to how their family has consciously and unconsciously taught them to see the world — to love within this world, and to interpret the actions of others — the more dependent they learn to be.

Unless this personalized system of cause and effect is broadened by the addition of other experiences, this personalized world view will become fixed and limiting as the people begin to form close relationships outside of the family. As they become wed to their particular view of the world and their place within it, they will fight anyone who attempts to counter it, for to change is to experience fear and to lose the perception of control. Power struggles often emerge when relationships are formed between two individuals from closed family systems, as two personal world views clash, and as each tries to defend against the anxiety represented by allowing in the other's viewpoint (Campbell, 1984).

... The Impact of Compulsive Dependency on Other Relationships

Seeing the world from only a personal perspective would work fine if you lived alone on a desert island. But it doesn't work in a relationship. Having children and attempting to parent together makes this difference in world view and the rules of loving apparent, even if it was not clear before. Children also complicate and intensify the power struggle, as they are watched to see whose view they will adopt, their mother's or father's, for in adopting one's parent's view, they also validate it.

Power Struggles and Addiction

The authors have found that those affected by addiction become engaged in power struggles by becoming trapped in a classic "triple bind." These tangled webs of attitudes about power were often unconsciously developed as a response to dealing with the crisis-orientation found in addicted families.

1. *Those affected by addiction can become fixed in the past.* They fear the past will repeat itself. Often they will inadvertently help recreate their past in their present, and in this way they put themselves in control of whatever may happen. Sometimes they need to know how well they will cope, and so they help create their own worst nightmares as a means of proving to themselves, and to others, that they will survive. Some have such high anxiety concerning what may happen, that they try to know ahead of time all that will occur by making it happen now.

2. *Or they may fear failure.* They fear that the future will not hold success for them, that their children will not progress, or that they will not grow. They feel cursed, that nothing will ever work out for them. They become caught in thinking and obsessing about all the terrible things that can happen, and planning how they will deal with them.

3. *Or they fear success.* They fear that they will have success and be forced to break with family tradition. They have great fear of being different, and rejected by their families. Often this bind becomes disguised as a fear of failure, for failure is more acceptable within the family system. But success is the real fear here. The hidden clue that this is occurring is when the person creates elaborate precautions in order to not allow success to be realized. If success occurs in spite of these precautions, it is minimized, not enjoyed or invalidated, for it is defined as fleeting.

When two people who have different and fixed worldviews form a relationship, power struggles emerge in these three ways. These personalized worldviews create conflicts for they define not only one's own actions, but also another's — specifically the spouse's or co-parent's. This results in couples not asking what is bothering the other, but assuming that they know not only what is going on, but why and whose fault it is. The clash of worldviews also results in not feeling loved, not feeling that one knows *how* to love one's spouse, or even one's children. Since there is little communication in the presence of power struggles there is much misinterpretation, and few if any opportunities for new input which would challenge these historic views.

Understanding the Power Struggle

"Either/or Thinking"

Power struggles develop from feeling that there can only be one winner. The type of reasoning that lies behind a power struggle is called "either/or thinking," for either you or your spouse must be right. There is no way for you both to be validated. Responsibility is not shared, just as in the family with active alcoholism. In fact, no one wants to assume responsibility, and so it is thrown about like a hot potato. Each party fights to exempt themselves from being wrong, and so must make the other wrong.

"When I could discuss anything with Diane," Matthew explains, "it was clear that only one of us could be right. Having kids made this crystal clear. Women in her family were 'always right' concerning 'the children.' Men in my family were 'always wrong,' and knew nothing about child-rearing. We were a perfect dysfunctional fit. When I decided that I didn't like this and needed to do something, I rebelled just like I did as a kid. I began to push for things that weren't even that important to me just because I didn't want to lose another round to her and be a wimp like my father, the passive alcoholic, was."

Developing "Both/and Thinking"

One way to resolve a power struggle is to move from "either/or thinking" to "both/and thinking." Including both points of view and taking the best from each is a way of stepping around a power struggle and re-defining the struggle from "win/lose" to "win/win" (Campbell, 1984).

"Not so easy to do, but possible," sighs Matthew. "Things were really getting out of hand with the kids, we had to do something. How did I do it? Really *we* did it." The authors have found that couples usually manage to negotiate their power struggles in the following manner:

1. Accept Your Spouse

Acceptance is crucial to redefining a power struggle. Acceptance is the essence of the first step of all 12-step recovery programs. Accept your spouse, you have made a commitment to him or her, and have gone through many rough times already. These difficult times have forged and strengthened your relationship, so if you can, let go and accept.

Matthew illustrates this: "I began to see Diane's need to define my role to not involve the kids, as a way of her remaining close to her family traditions which said 'don't trust men around children.' This made sense when I remembered that she was an incest victim. Instead of always being angry at her, I began to see her great love of our children, and to deeply appreciate her need to protect them. In accepting her I realized that I did love her, something that in my righteous anger I had lost sight of. In my family, love was always replaced by anger. It occurred to me that I had been carrying on that tradition."

2. Change Your Interpretations of Your Spouse's Actions

You can only change yourself. Begin by owning your personal view of the world and be willing to entertain your spouse's. This small step will produce a marked change in your relationship.

Matthew again elaborates: "I realized that I couldn't change her, and maybe I didn't have to if I could see what was really motivating her, instead of judging her from my point of view. First I changed how I interpreted her actions. These same actions under a different banner heading seemed fine. A bit quirky, but that's Diane.

"Next I accepted her and released her from my constant judging of her. Interestingly as I backed off, Diane became more verbal about her worries about the children and acted them out less. I became less of the enemy, which meant, of course, that I had to be willing to give up this role, and risk getting closer to Diane. To give up my role I first had to realize I had the power to change myself."

3. Change Your Own Actions

After you have realized the legitimacy of your spouse's view, you can decide what you want to do, knowing that you have the power to change yourself. This means taking responsibility for yourself, and yourself alone. Not an easy task, as Matthew observes:

"How to change me? It was easier to do after I stopped putting all my energy into changing her. I began with how I reacted around the kids. I accepted Diane's need to protect them. But I stopped acting so inadequate around them, like my father had. This meant that I stopped sending Diane the message that I couldn't handle them, and that they needed to be protected from my bumbling. My changing my actions, and accepting hers, resulted in a big change. We stopped battling so much. We moved from 'either/or thinking' to 'both/and thinking.' It is great to be in a relationship where you both emerge as winners.''

Some Guidelines for Moving Beyond the Power Struggle

Once you have negotiated the power struggle, you need to recommit to each other. Commitment can be a challenge, for it involves learning some new behaviors. But this can be seen as the next necessary step in the life-long process of recovery.

Develop 'Active Listening' Skills

- Train yourself to actively listen to the feelings of your life partner before you respond. If it is unclear, ask.
- Actively learn more about your partner — her fears, hopes and insights regarding your children, your marriage, herself.

Plan Time Together

- Plan time to be together away from the children. Even an hour here or there can work wonders.
- Pick up a weekly time to review issues which concern the children. Let at least part of this time be away from the children.

Negotiate Differences

- Respect the different values of your husband or wife. After all, if you agreed on everything, you would be the same person.
- If a decision is not as important to you as it is to your spouse, let it pass. Let him or her have it their way. And don't go back and say "I told you so" when there are problems.
- Learn to defer judgment on a problem if you are too tired to process it.

Develop Clear Expectations Together for:
1. Your children regarding:
   - appropriate behavior
   - expected behavior, i.e., chores
   - the consequences for inappropriate behavior
   - rewards
   - other ways to motivate your children.
2. Yourself as a parent regarding:
   - what role each of you is willing to play with the children.
3. Yourselves as a couple, paying close attention to:
   - what translates into love for each of you
   - how to show your partner, in a way that he or she understands, that they are loved.

Negotiating power issues is not a one-time event, and it is never easy. You will need to pay constant attention to this area of your development. Remember, growth is not linear. You will go back and forth, and have spurts and setbacks. Even trees do not grow even bands each year. So be gentle with each other as you grow and love together.

Parenting Alone

Sometimes recovery can involve stays in alcoholism rehabilitation facilities which are not close to home. At other times the effects of the disease can result in separation, divorce or even death. This means learning to parent alone.

Losing a husband or wife, even temporarily, only deprives you of the opportunity of working through problems in the presence of your spouse. Old problems do not just evaporate. Power struggles which were never resolved with your spouse still need to be resolved within yourself. And not only have you been affected by power struggles, but so have your children.

Parenting alone presents the same issues as parenting with a spouse. Certainly the child's developmental issues are the same. The child needs the same amount of structure, support and consistency (see Part II: As They Grow). The difference is that you are now only one, as opposed to two, trying to provide for your children.

You need *support, support,* and more *support.* Not only do you need this support but you deserve it as well. There can be many sources for support. They range, depending on your need, from family week or day programs at the alcoholism treatment facility, to professional help, to your 12-step program, where the topic of parenting alone would spark a lively discussion, to other self-help organizations, such as Parents Without Partners.

Remember that living with alcoholism and other addictions teaches one to live alone. You need to break free of this and reach out to others. Don't isolate yourself or your children.

Blended Families

As we know separation, divorce and death of a spouse are common in families ravaged by alcoholism. This results in a high number of remarriages and live-in arrangements. When children are present, these are called *blended families*, as each adult represents a parental figure.

This need not mean that the child calls both women "Mother," or both men "Father." A child will often resist that with good cause. It does mean that the child now has more adults to love and to please in his or her life. Loyalties may become divided and painful for the child, particularly when biological parents are involved in power struggles. It is important to remember that even when parents are not outwardly struggling, a child feels torn. On one level he wants "Mommy" and "Daddy" to be back together. This is a normal, irrational (at least from the parents' point of view) and largely unconscious desire by the child, which needs to be accepted by the adults in his or her life.

Divorce, where children are involved, is marriage by another name, for now a life-long relationship exists with the ex-spouse through the children. Parenting under these circumstances is difficult. But not because the child wants it to be. It is unavoidable for there are just that many more people involved in the child's life, and that many more people involved in yours.

Everything that has been said about the power struggles occurring within a marriage goes double for a blended family. Eliminating these power struggles and working to develop communication are crucial if harmony within the family and within the marriage is to be established.

Special Issues

Some special issues within the blended family need to be addressed. These again are issues of power struggles compounded by guilt. The authors have found these issues can be addressed successfully, once they are understood.

1. Double Standards

There should not be two sets of standards, one for those children who reside with you, and one for those children who spend weekends and/or summers. This is difficult to accomplish, but necessary. There must be rules for all the children to follow, and rewards and consequences (for more on this, see Part II). It is recommended that the rules govern expectations that occur only during the time the child is with you. The issue here is that the behavior and its accompanying rewards and consequences must be able to be accomplished over the weekend or summer.

For example, taking away bike riding for a month for a child who only spends every other weekend with you is not a good idea. When the child returns in two weeks, having ridden his bike at the other parent's home in between, your grounding him will seem more mean, than meaningful, as too much time will have elapsed.

In cases of serious behavioral problems, for example in the case of a child arrested for burglary, and where there is a good relationship between the separated parents, exception can be made, and punishment can be coordinated between the two sets of parents. But you and the child must be very clear as to what this exception is and why it is happening.

2. Who Is In Charge?

Another complication that arises when a child has double parents, and parents have double sets of children, is who makes the rules for which children? Who is in charge? In some families power can be shared, even with the children. Here the parenting as a team approach can and does work well. In other families, frequently guilt, or apathy on the part of the non-biological parent, interferes, and only the biological parent makes the rules or enforces them with their children.

To determine which style will work for you, you need to have some serious conversations with your partner. It is recommended that you try to clarify who has the role with what children. This will not only help you, but it makes that child's life easier and more secure as well. For a child, security comes from predictability.

Summary

Learning to be a good parent can be part of the recovery process. Parenting as a team means working through power struggles found within the marriage, and then getting down to the business of negotiating how to be the parent that your children need, and that you would like to be. The separation, permanent or temporary, of a spouse and the blending of families, only compounds power struggles. Acceptance of your spouse and yourself provides the important first steps in re-negotiating power issues.

PART II
As They Grow

Chapter 5

Preparing for Birth and Parenting the Infant

"Today I brought my son Tim to the babysitter. He was crying. He started his day so upset. I vowed that if I ever became a parent that I would never do to my child what my parents did to me. Why? Why am I doing just what I was afraid I would do?" asks Maggie, 32, an adult child of an alcoholic and an active alcoholic and prescription drug abuser, married to Gary, son of an alcoholic who was also a compulsive gambler.

Preparing for Birth

Just making the decision to have a child raises anxiety in those who have been affected by alcoholism and other addictions. Being pregnant raises yet additional concerns. How to prepare for a coming child? You can increase the likelihood of having a healthy baby by:

- following a healthy diet, no binging or purging,
- not drinking alcohol or caffeine,
- not using illicit drugs or nicotine,
- not misusing any prescription or over-the-counter drugs;
- following a healthy exercise program.

No single action will ensure the health of your baby, but by stopping alcohol use, drug abuse, caffeine and nicotine use, and eating healthy foods in a responsible manner, you will know that you are doing everything that is possible to help your baby. It is important to remember that no one can guarantee the health of your baby. Genetics and age of the parents are also important variables in determining the health of your child (Russell, 1982). All we are speaking about here is controlling what is in your power to control — not an insignificant task for recovering people.

Aside from proper diet and exercise, reading and speaking to other parents will help prepare you for what might occur. In preparing for birth you need to have faith in yourself and your partner and in your support programs. Learn to relax and enjoy the process, and after the child is born, follow the simple rules outlined in this chapter.

Parenting Infants and Addiction

Taking care of an infant can feel like an overwhelming task for someone who has been affected by alcoholism. Infants are so fragile and require so much time and attention that the very purity of their vulnerability can strike fear, resentment and feelings of inadequacy in a mother or father who did not receive adequate care themselves.

As Maggie illustrates: "I feel sometimes that I have been cursed by my family. When I had my first child and asked my mother for help, she said, 'You'll learn.' But she never told me how to care for my baby. Didn't she realize that I had no experience to draw upon? I had to do this all alone just like I grew up, all alone. I resented it and, God forgive me, at times I also resented my child. If Tim didn't get my wrath, Gary, my husband, would."

The Young Infant – Under Six Months

Rule: Parents need to provide their infant with a calm, predictable, consistent and loving environment.

Infants require consistency, love and a calm and predictable environment (Mussen, Conger, Kagan, 1969). This may seem like a tall order and for some of you, an impossible one. Let's look at each one of these needs separately.

Parenting Guidelines

Predictability is not rigidity. Predictability for infants means learning that when they cry, they will be comforted. This does not mean that comfort must come immediately or even every time. There are valid philosophies of child-rearing, for example, that state that it may be appropriate for infants of a certain age to cry themselves to sleep after they have been fed and changed. Predictability only means that the child can look forward to being comforted and develop an expectation that it will occur.

Consistency is also not rigidity. It does not mean that every time an infant is comforted, it must be done the same way. Consistency means that there are limits that the nurturing falls within, and that it *always* falls within these limits.

Calm is not the absence of stimulation. Calm is stimulation which the child can absorb, stimulation that does not overpower the child and frighten him or her. Children are very adaptable. They can get used to different levels of stimulation. How much stimulation a child needs depends in part on the personality present at birth. It also depends on the normal activity level of their family. To have a totally calm environment is impossible. Doors will slam, voices may occasionally be raised. This is normal. It is nonetheless important to strive to have a calm environment.

It is very difficult not to love an infant. It is, however, possible to have difficulty in showing your love. Part of this difficulty may come from feelings of competition with one's child.

Gary admits, "I used to feel that this kid had a lot more than I did. It would make me feel sad. Sad for *me.* I began to wish that I had had me for a father. I began to resent that Tim had it so good. This really got in the way of how I cared for Timmy, until I realized what was going on."

It is important to remember that love can be shown in many ways that we sometimes do not think of as loving. A smile, a laugh, a bottle full of warm milk, a toy, a touch — all are ways we show we love. However timidly we express them, our feelings are not lost on the infant. Infants process the world through their feelings. They can sense yours. Conscious and cognitive thoughts, as we shall see, come later.

Given this world of love, relative calm, predictability and consistency, the infant sets about to accomplish his development. One of the first tasks that the infant learns is how to alleviate the pain of hunger. Instinctively, infants vocalize and move about. Eventually they learn that they can produce an end to their hunger pains by these actions. This is a crucial point. The infant is learning that he or she can reduce their pain and influence their world. This is the beginning of the child's developing a sense of mastery over himself and his environment.

By nurturing the child, the mother and father bond to the child, and the infant, in turn, bonds with its parents. Bonding is important for both the parent and the child. Bonding allows the child to feel secure. Security for the infant is experienced as a sense of order and predictability. Bonding allows the parents to begin to feel that they know what they are doing, to develop a sense of mastery which will be the cornerstone of their later parenting. Bonding with a child also allows a parent to feel that the commitment they have made to the child is worthwhile. After all, parenting is hard work. If you don't feel close to your child, it makes it much more difficult.

The Impact of Addiction

Love, consistency and predictability are the important parenting tasks. The very nature of alcoholism makes following this rule difficult. Alcoholism causes personality changes which result in parents not being predictable (Wallace, 1985). Emotional blow-ups within the family can shatter the calm that all parents would like to be able to give their child (Nardi, 1981).

What alcoholism does not affect, however, is the love the parent has for their child. It only affects how this love is demonstrated. The devastating part of alcoholism is that it robs both parent and child. Alcoholic parents are robbed of feelings of mastery and competence. They are also denied an outlet for their love.

Children are affected by alcoholism on many levels. Infants often have difficulty being calm and anticipating that their needs will be met. This means learning to trust. Trust is not an all-or-nothing phenomenon. Just because a child comes from a home with alcoholism does not mean that he or she is scarred for life. It just means that certain tasks will be more difficult. For example, learning to trust.

As noted in the previous chapter, children do learn to trust. To not trust and to be an infant means to die. We saw this in studies of English children separated from their parents for months during World War II. Here large numbers of otherwise healthy infants died for they had no hope. They received virtually no individual love, no touching, no cuddling; predictable or not. They gave up and died (Spitz, Wolf, 1946). This is the extreme. No one reading this book fell into this category or you would not be here today.

The infant is resilient. The infants fights to live, to grow, to master, even when the odds are against him. Despite intermittent caring, and ravages of wars, famine and natural disasters, children can and do survive and thrive. Children in these situations, which some have likened to growing up in an alcoholic home, do learn to trust. But they learn a different type of trust, a trust where the verdict is out longer as to whether trust has been earned. It consequently takes longer to see if trust will be granted. Others may learn to trust only themselves, excluding others as untrustworthy. This may lead to later anti-social behavior (Mussen, Conger, Kagan, 1969).

For children of alcoholics, difficulty in trusting and in the relative lack of calm has ramifications for later life.

As Maggie tells us: "I felt so inadequate in trying to give my children something I had not experienced. Somehow I felt like a fake. I acted calm, but inside I was terrified. I prayed that it wouldn't show. One thing I am proud of is that somehow I did manage to be predictable, at least when Tim was an infant."

Remember, both parents do not have to be available at the same time for the child to grow. Even if your husband or wife cannot be a more predictable, consistent, calm or outwardly loving parent, you should not give up. Do the best you can to achieve these goals. Children are adaptable. All a child minimally needs is one caretaker at a time. Yes, this does put an added stress on the more consistent caretaker, but this stress can be managed with support from 12-step programs, friends and family.

Rule: Parenting is trial and error.

There is no easy way to learn to be a parent. This is hard for perfectionists to accept. Not knowing for someone who has been affected by alcoholism usually increases anxiety. You need to learn that you will not have all the answers ahead of time. No parent does.

The Importance of Information

Several tried-and-true methods have been developed over generations to reduce the natural anxiety of parenting. Information gathering is one way. Reading about parenting will provide you with some of the basics. Experience also helps. Even if you grew up in an alcoholic home, your previous experience with young children can quell some of your anxiety. Finding a support network is another important means of not only gathering information, but also support and assistance. This is why in many cultures a married women lives close to her mother. Her mother and other female family members are there with the knowledge and support she needs to help rear her child. The rule to be learned here is do not isolate yourself. But this is easier said than done when you have learned to live with alcoholism. It may require you to break family tradition to reach out to other mothers and fathers and develop friendships. Make the effort.

By obtaining information from your doctor, friends or other authorities, you can test your reactions to some classic situations, such as preparing for childbirth.

Learning From Your Baby

Responses to infants are learned (Bower, 1977). It is common to over-react to your infant in the beginning, when you are tired or under stress. It is also common to under-react, only to find out later that your baby has kicked off all the covers and is cold and crying. Your reactions to your infant will never be perfect, so there is no reason to feel guilty when you discover a missing cover, or a cut or a bruise. What is important is how you handle the situation, not how you were inadvertently responsible for it. Many new parents are tempted to feel eternal guilt. Watch this pattern of guilt as it is probably more reflective of your overall personality style than it is an appropriate response to the situation. You may also want to try to check this reaction early so that you do not sow the seeds for your taking on too much responsibility. Learning from your children means learning to forgive yourself.

Mothers who begin to know their children can often predict and interpret their early non-verbal behavior. Often mothers and fathers, who are primary caretakers, will begin to tell that their baby is hungry or needs to be changed just by a change of tone in a cry, or a subtle action on their baby's part. This knowledge if based on trial and error, spending time with the child and frequently misinterpreting their infant's communications until a pattern is discerned.

Most of what you will learn about yourself as a parent and your child will come from actual experience and from your ability to learn from your experiences. Being spontaneous and not taking yourself too seriously are important lessons. Once you begin to become freer with your experiences and less judgmental, you will be able to interact more with your infant and enjoy him or her more. Learning more about your baby and yourself also promotes parent-child bonding. As you get closer to your child and understand your manner of responding and fulfilling his or her needs, you can begin to develop more self-confidence.

The Impact of Addiction

Diseases such as alcoholism unfortunately interfere with this natural trial-and-error learning. For the person who is under the influence, experiences do not usually result in learning (Wallace, 1985). Consequently, the mastery of parenting tasks is delayed. For example, learning to predict why the baby is crying will take longer. This results in increased stress for the child and parent and an increase in the length of time it will take the child to bond with their caretaking parent (McCall, 1979).

For the spouse of an alcoholic, learning is also interfered with as the alcoholic's neediness conflicts with the needs of their child (see Chapter 9). Children's needs will be less consistently dealt with, again delaying the parents getting to know and care for their child.

The adult child of an alcoholic presents a different dilemma. These parents may tend to doubt their ability to learn. They tend to be over-anxious parents who are afraid that they will miss something with their child. They often become hyper-attentive (Black, 1981; Gravitz, Bowden, 1985). In fact, they are so attentive that they miss quite a bit by creating such an air of anxiety that the child will sense this and respond to the anxiety instead of the parent.

Martin, 24, has been married for two years and has a two-month-old girl. Martin is the adult child of an alcoholic and suffers from being a compulsive overeater. Many of the arguments he has with Lisa, his wife, have to do with his anxiety concerning Glynnis, their daughter. The fact that she is thriving and growing on breast milk is not enough for Marty. He goes with Lisa to doctor appointments so that he can personally ask the questions which keep him awake and eating until all hours of the night. Gradually Marty is learning what is normal for Glynnis. Lisa is also beginning to learn that Marty's questioning of her stems from his anxiety, and is not a comment on her mothering.

She says, "If we ever have another child, it will be easier, for at least I won't personalize all of Marty's insecurities. At least I hope I won't."

Food preferences are another area of potential anxiety (McCall, 1979). When solid food is introduced and definite preferences emerge, anxiety may increase. Gradually, by trial and error, you will learn your child's preferences (hopefully before they change them on you again). Anxiety over food can be subtly transmitted. Try to avoid seeing rejection of food as rejection of the food provider: just because your child is rejecting strained peaches does not mean she is rejecting you.

Alcoholism and related problems have a tendency to affect parents by making them feel that they must be perfect (Black, 1981). "I feared that if I didn't do everything just right, Tim would grow up to be a mess," sighs Maggie. Be reassured no parent is or can be perfect.

Better to put your energies into enjoying your baby and delighting in her and your accomplishments, than directing all your energies into mulling over the way you were raised.

The Older Infant — 6 to 8 Months

As a child grows he begins to assert what he wants. Not only do children have distinct preferences, but they begin to change physically and to look distinctive. Parents begin to realize that they are dealing with another person, which may mean a loss of control.

As Maggie relates: "Changes were gradual with Tim. Then one day I realized that he wasn't just a doll for me to feed and put to bed. He was beginning to talk. He recognized me, was afraid of strangers, and wouldn't smile on command. I got scared all over again. I felt again that I wasn't in as much control as I needed to be."

Rule: Parents need to accept that children of both sexes will probably have an initial strong bond with their mothers.

The reason for this is that the mother tends to be the primary caretaker and is the first person the child can depend upon and communicate with to have basic needs met. Since most of the comforting and nurturing has been provided by the mother, when the child is upset, she will seek out the parent she knows will understand and take care of her. This changes as the child gets older and has more experiences with the father and other adult caretakers. But it is important to remember that this early attachment is natural and normal, and not a statement concerning who is the better or favored parent. It is a statement only on who is more familiar to the child and whom the child can communicate with more readily (Schaeffer, 1971).

The Impact of Addiction

Maggie, the adult child of alcoholic parents, helps us see that this mother/child bond can be double-edged: "I felt so actively ambivalent with Tim's strong ties to me. Part of me felt great. I was so important to him. That meant I was important. But since I 'X'ed Gary out of Tim's life for 'I was the one,' I also felt overwhelmed and without support."

. . . The Impact on the Father

A child's strong ties with his mother can set up dynamics with far-reaching ripples within the alcoholic family. Fathers often have a difficult time with young children. Part of the reason is the trouble some men have in delighting in a pre-verbal, dependent being.

Gary explains: "There just wasn't enough of a person there for me to interact with and feel satisfied. I also was so frightened that I could hurt him. But that was just part of the reason I had a difficult time with Tim. I also felt rejected because Maggie and Tim seemed to have their 'thing' going and I was excluded.

"For a long time whenever Tim cried, only Maggie could comfort him. I felt useless and left out just like when I was a kid. When Maggie began to drink more heavily, I didn't know what to do since I wasn't part of their world anyway so I withdrew."

This normal process of a close bonding between mother and child also results at times in the inability of fathers to show as much initiative in caring for children. While some women have little difficulty with this in the beginning, after the child is older and the father is still not actively involved, resentments emerge concerning the mother's feelings that she has to "do it all."

The parent with active addiction also has difficulty with this phase of parenting. An alcoholic father may see child's natural initial preference for mother as a rejection of him, and not as a natural phase of development. He may later feel guilty in recovery that somehow he caused this natural event to occur. His wife may feel the same resentments and fears expressed by Maggie — power, but with too much responsibility. An alcoholic mother may experience this child's dependence on her as excessive. This dependence may heighten her sense of inadequacy that she has to pretend to know what to do. Her fear is that if she somehow falters, the world will cave in. This fear and lack of other ways of negotiating it may even lead her to greater alcohol use to deaden her fears, as it did with Maggie.

The mother/child bonding may contribute to adult children of an alcoholic feeling that they have to do everything and do it alone.

"Somehow being a mother made me again feel if I didn't do it, it wouldn't get done," says Maggie. "Suddenly I had to control everything all over again. Gary just wasn't there. And I blamed him for leaving me hanging. What I wasn't aware of was that I had pushed Gary away. I hadn't helped him create a role with Tim, particularly when Tim would only be comforted by me. I see now that I should have at least asked

Gary to comfort *me*. I loved being so powerful with Tim, yet I resented both Tim and Gary for the enormity of the responsibility I felt."

Enjoying Your Baby

Having a baby is a mutual responsibility. How you choose to divide child care will depend on your other priorities. The important issue is to decide who is going to do what with your baby. The following are some guidelines to assist you:

1. Decide together who has certain child care tasks.
2. Try to take turns in doing some aspect of child care.
3. Share your experiences and those of your infant with one another.
4. If there are older children, let their care be as important as your infant's. If they are old enough, see if they can safely participate in some safe aspect of infant care.
5. Remember, you will learn as you go if you get the support that you need.
6. If resentments develop because you believe your infant will have a better life than you because they have you as a parent, do some parenting to yourself. Be good to yourself and you will have fewer times of resenting your baby. If resentments persist, you may want to speak to a professional.

Love your baby as much as you can. There is no limit to the amount of love that a baby can absorb.

Summary

Parenting is a learned skill. No one was born to be a parent. Skillful parenting is developed out of trial and error. This means you will make mistakes and need to learn to forgive yourself. Remember that you cannot do it all at once. Familial alcoholism may have influenced the development of your parenting skills, but it does not have to affect your ability to learn or to love. As you try some new techniques, don't try to be perfect. It is impossible and a waste of time. Better to put your energy into enjoying and loving your baby and appreciating his or her accomplishments: learning to walk, to speak, to be like Mommy and Daddy. Enjoy your ability to give to your child, and celebrate your mastery over what you have needed to overcome to get here.

Chapter 6

Parenting the Toddler and Pre-school Child

"Glynnis is so ambivalent. One minute she wants me, and then she would push me away and have a temper tantrum when I went near her. I felt like such a failure," says Lisa, age 23, an adult child of an alcoholic, and bulimic herself.

Parenting the Toddler — 18 months to 3 years

The toddler is an emerging autonomous person. Not only are they now learning to move on their own, but toddlers are also learning to express themselves verbally, beginning to deal with their need for independence and learning to control their bodily functions. Gone is the very special relationship where only the mother knew what the child wanted or needed and where only the mother could comfort the child. The child may now go to either parent for comforting, although there will still be a mother-first preference noted. The toddler makes his or her desires known, at times more than the parents wish, hence the term "terrible twos."

Rule: Parents need to foster their child's need for independence.

The toddler is highly ambivalent, reflecting difficulty of moving from dependence on one person, a mother, to self-sufficiency (Crowe, 1980).

"When I think of Tim moving to be self-sufficient, I'm really amazed. I feel I haven't yet completed this process, and I know Maggie hasn't," states Gary, whose father was an alcoholic and a compulsive gambler.

For the toddler, there is a push/pull quality to feelings of dependence. Sometimes it is OK. And sometimes it is not. The toddler dramatically exhibits this by running over to his mother to be comforted and when she goes to comfort her child, she may be pushed away. The toddler wants and doesn't want to be independent. He or she is experimenting with how different responses feel and how successful one response is over another in meeting his or her needs.

The Development of Compulsive Dependency

Again, consistency on the part of the parents is important, particularly when the child is inconsistent. The child needs to know that he will not be punished for wanting to do things on his own. If parents are inconsistent during this period, the child may well develop excessive dependency needs. Probably the easiest way to ensure the development of excessive dependence in a child is to reward an activity one time and punish it the next (Mussen, Conger, Kagan, 1969).

The Impact of Addiction

This is unfortunately the case in the family where there is alcoholism and other active addictions. The lack of predictability for the consequences of actions is important. For example, a child may be punished for sucking his thumb by a parent under the influence. The other parent may encourage the child to suck his thumb when the parent is intoxicated as a way of having the child reduce his or her stress. The same activity when the parent is not intoxicated may go unnoticed by both parents.

This, in the authors' experience, is the reason why adult children of alcoholics who feel so frightened by independence often develop compulsively dependent relationships. ACoAs reason that if you are dependent on someone else, then you do not need to risk being vulnerable and potentially punished for your own decisions. If you are never making decisions for yourself but are only making decisions for others, then you can be safe.

For the active alcoholic or addicted parent encouraging independence is also difficult for this taps into the alcoholic's own ambivalence over his lack of independence from alcohol (Wallace, 1985). Active alcoholics have not yet decided that they want independence. Encouraging independence in the toddler by the compulsively dependent person is also difficult. The compulsively dependent parent has a great need to be needed even if the need is overwhelming at times. The trade-off for not being needed, but allowing their child to be more independent, may not be worth it to them because of the secondary gains attached.

"This for me was the real trap of motherhood," Maggie recalls. "I could always couch my feelings and decision in terms of what was best for Tim. I didn't have to decide what was best for me. I think at times I depended on Tim more than that little fellow could ever have depended on me."

And yet parents do learn how to encourage these skills of independence. Sometimes the child may learn later than other children but most do learn if encouraged. In learning, the child attains mastery.

Remember that with any developmental benchmark there is a range of time in which it is normal for a child to learn a specific task, whether it is drinking from a cup or learning to tie his shoes. At whatever point you appropriately encourage a task, learning can begin (Crowe, 1980).

Marty sums this up: "When I realized that it wasn't too late to encourage Glynnis to be independent, I felt a great relief. Maybe I hadn't screwed up her life after all."

Rule: Parents need to enourage children to develop control over their impulses.

Toilet training, masturbation and aggression represent singly difficult issues for most parents. Yet they all begin to be issues for both parent and child during the toddler stage. Their combined effect can create a greater degree of intensity and anxiety in the parent than each of these issues would generate if dealt with separately (Chess, Thomas, Birch, 1976).

Unfortunately, they all come at once. No parent has the luxury of dealing with only one of these at a time. These developmental issues are difficult for many parents because they also tap into areas which remain unresolved to some degree in their own lives, particularly if alcoholism was present during their childhoods.

Toilet Training

Children want to be like the adults who surround them, and to master the tasks that they see the adults around them perform. Boys and girls want to go to the bathroom like they see Mommy and Daddy do. They want to get out of diapers and wear underwear like big people. They are just not sure how to go about it. They need adult guidance and encouragement, positive guidance, clear and consistent encouragement, to develop a sense of control.

This means that each child will be working on his or her own timetable, not yours. When the child's timetable is interfered with, there can be problems.

Gary recalls his mother, who was married to an alcoholic compulsive gambler: "I never learned to wipe myself until I started the first grade. I remember my mother saying to call her and I did. I feel weird now thinking of how dependent I was on her and how dependent she was on me. It has taken me a longer time than most to learn to care for myself."

Masturbation

Children enjoy the pleasure that their bodies bring them (Erikson, 1963). When they touch their genitals in public or with the family present they are not trying to be provocative. Children do not have an adult sense of sexuality. They do not know what intercourse is. They are just touching a part of their bodies that makes them feel good, much like they would suck their thumbs.

Often when children touch themselves, it is a sign that something is amiss. They may be tired or bored and are trying to take care of their own needs by giving themselves pleasure. Parents have discovered many ways of dealing with this, from asking the child if she is tired or hungry, to distracting her, to telling the older toddler that he can touch himself in his room but not in front of company.

"It was difficult for me to gently and non-judgmentally tell Glynnis when she was five that she could go to her room, but that we as a family did not touch our privates in public," sighs Marty.

"Once Lisa and I started to establish what our family rules were going to be, it got easier. We talked it through and realized that even though we were both impulsive, we didn't want Glynnis to be quite that way."

Children will often mimic what they see (Bandura, 1963). The child will learn by watching what behaviors their parents model. They will be likely to imitate what they see, for that is how they learn. For example, if sexual activity occurs in front of a child, he or she will be stimulated and curious. But they will not know what they are doing even if they attempt to do the same as they saw. Remember, children are mimics.

Children need as much protection as it is possible to provide. Closing bedrooms doors, and keeping the sounds that accompany sexual intercourse low are obvious but necessary ways of protecting the child.

Aggression

We have found that aggression is another difficult issue for parents to deal with, particularly within a family affected by alcoholism, because anger is so often an issue. Children need to learn the safe bounds of their anger. Sometimes for the toddler, a loud "no!" or a swift and gentle whack on the behind is sufficient to get them to learn that they cannot throw a dangerous object at another person. Later, this "no" or whack may need to be repeated or threatened. This is normal. Sometimes children of alcoholics have difficulty setting limits (Ackerman, 1983).

"I would feel so guilty if I even yelled at Tim that I would hate myself," Maggie moans. Yet discipline is important if a child is to learn.

. . . In a Home With Abuse

In a home where there is frequent verbal and physical aggression children will often act out what they see, frequently with the same person who received the abuse. For example, in an alcoholic home with physical violence where a mother is hit, it is not uncommon for a young child to also hit his mother. The child is mimicking what he has seen, and may be experimenting with how one deals with anger by using his mother as a safe target.

In this situation the child needs to learn that he cannot hit his mother. A loud "No!" may be enough to get this point across. It's also important in such a home for mother not to take all or even part of the anger she has towards her husband out on her child. It's better to discuss it, rather than to overly react to your child. This does not mean don't react and "just take it," but if you choose to discipline your child, discipline your child and not your husband in your child's guise, and do so in an appropriate and non-malicious way.

If the child is the target of verbal or physical abuse, it is important that he or she be comforted. Children will normally feel that they have caused abuse. Children at this age feel that they are the center of the universe, and that all actions that concern them are a result of their actions and thoughts (Ginnot, 1965). If possible, the abusing parent needs to apologize to the child. The child needs to receive the clear message that the abusing parent is truly sorry and loves the child, even though the parent has a problem in showing this love. At all costs it is important to tell and reassure the child that he or she did not cause the uproar, and that they did not deserve the abuse.

Parenting The Pre-school Child — Age 3 to 5 years

The pre-school child is now talking, probably toilet-trained and ready to set about learning another set of tasks. The next challenge for pre-schoolers is to learn about socializing in groups and within the family. To do this children need to begin to develop some understanding of how they feel. Not only will children be expressing feelings, but they will also begin to recognize how and why they have certain feelings. To accomplish this the child begins by developing rudimentary concepts of "good" and "bad." This complements their growing understanding of their own motivation (Rosen, 1980). Remember this is only a beginning. The child does not have adult concepts of right and wrong. It is only during this developmental stage that these concepts begin to emerge.

The Impact of Addiction
. . . The Perfectionist Child

As the child begins to mature, a problem that crops up in homes with alcoholism is that parents can begin to expect too much too soon. Since the child is beginning to have the initial stirrings of adult concepts, some parents expect that the child will be there sooner than is developmentally possible. All children are highly adaptive. If the expectation level is too high within the family, the child will experience repeated failure to meet parental expectations. This is where children begin to internalize, judging themselves by standards which are too high (Chess, Thomas, Birch, 1976). There are two equally rigid outcomes to this extreme — either the child will become a perfectionist and feel inadequate, or he will give up and not try for he can never measure up to his parents' unrealistic expectations. Either extreme portends problems for both the child and the family. The perfectionist child frequently will become obsessed with performing. The child who has given up will frequently become depressed and may later act out his frustration, or withdraw completely.

. . . *The Parental Child*

The family tradition of perfectionism can be passed down from one generation to another (Papp, 1983). In the family with alcoholism this is usually accomplished by making children into parents. The child strives to be like her parent and to do this she must do everything right. Once children are put in parental roles, they try their hardest to fulfill the perceived expectations of their family. They attempt to take care of their parents as opposed to socialize with them. The two become synonymous; to be social is to take care. Since learning to socialize is the basic developmental task, the child will devise some ingenious ways to accomplish it.

In the family with alcoholism the child can also be easily slid into a premature adult role (O'Gorman, 1974; Nardi, 1981).

Gary recalls trying to control how much his father drank:

"My heart would break seeing my father drink. Here I was age five and crying, telling my father that I didn't want him to die, and please not to drink so much. My mother later told me that she could hear her own words pointed back at her. Somehow I had associated drinking with dying. Mom said that she knew then that we had some serious problems ahead, but she didn't know what to do about it."

Maggie recalls her early childhood: "I was the little miss, the little princess, but what this really meant was that I was an adult and no longer a child. I feel sometimes that my childhood ended as soon as I could walk and talk. My parents tell me what a cute baby I was, but after that they are vague about my childhood. I remember around age four trying to get their approval on whatever I did. I don't remember if they ever complimented me. I feel like my whole life I have been striving to get 'my parents' in the guise of my boss or even my husband to say I've done well. Sometimes I even put my five-year-old Tim in that role and hang on to his approval. I know it's a bit of a role reversal but I still get stuck."

. . . *The Acting-out Child*

Even when children have given up trying to please their parents, they are still in subtle ways trying to take care of them (O'Gorman, Ross, 1986). A child may take care by either keeping out of the way or by offering himself as a problem via his troublesome behavior. This is often an attempt, the authors have found, for the child to unite the family and hence care for his parents. Enlightened family therapists are able to begin to see this pattern.

Such enlightenment in family therapy is recent. Says Gary, "I remember my family going into counseling just before I started the first grade. I wasn't fully toilet trained, and I couldn't stand being away from my mother. I would also break things, lots of things, on purpose. There was a real concern about whether or not I could begin first grade. Looking back on it now, I realize that I was trying to keep my father home and involved with my family.

"My mother would cry about Dad being gone, and then she would pretend that everything was all right. But I knew he was drinking and he would die. Only when I was older, did I find out that when he was not home, he was also gambling. I knew how to get him home and that was to tear up the place. Unfortunately my behavior was always the focus of therapy. We were in therapy off and on for years. They never dealt with Dad's drinking or gambling, or my attempt to parent my mom and bring my dad home. I wish there had been Gamblers Anonymous for my father back then. Maybe he would have joined. But he never joined AA so I guess I'm just wishing it could have been different."

Allowing Your Child to be a Child

As easy as it is to have a child assume an adult role, it is also possible to begin to move a child back into a child's role. Children need to know that their parents are in charge and can manage their lives. Children need to feel cared about and protected. To allow your child to be a child, start treating him or her like one. Tell them how much you love them. Remove excess responsibilities. Expect your child to act like a child and not like an adult. There is plenty of time for them to be adults later. This does not mean that your children will not react to your trying to change their roles, as we have learned already from Leann and others (see Chapter 2). They will react by doing things the old way until they realize that this change is safe.

Guidelines

1. Don't bring adult concerns to your child no matter how mature they seem. They shouldn't have to know that there is little money, or that Daddy puts too much pressure on Mommy to have sex. They also should not be asked to protect one parent from another.
2. Do have child-based rituals. Have a play time with your child. If this is a problem for you, play an organized game with your child.

Try to let your imagination join your child's and have fun together. Read your child to sleep at night. It can be just one short story. Have a night-time ritual that is predictable — a story, a kiss and an "I love you." It is important for your child to sleep in the security of your love. Have the day begin in a way that is predictable. For example, you and your child always having breakfast together.

3. Don't get into power battles with your toddler. Don't just say "no" to get your point across, use short phrases.

4. Don't sleep with your child unless the circumstance is unusual, i.e., they have had a nightmare, or are ill. Sleeping with your children will only teach them to depend on you unnecessarily.

5. Don't be over-anxious. If your toddler is having a temper tantrum and is safe, tell him that you'll talk about it when he calms down, and walk away.

6. Do guide your child toward independence. Realize that when a child says "no," he or she is proclaiming separateness. Don't over-react.

7. Answer any and all questions your child asks concerning sex, alcoholism, etc. Give short responses. If they don't understand, they'll ask again. Read materials designed to help you speak to your children about these issues. (See *Suggested Reading* list at the end of this book.)

8. Be consistent. As soon as you find something positive that works, keep using it.

9. Do keep telling your child how much you love them.

Summary

Parenting is a learned skill. These skills can be acquired and implemented while they are still developing. Parenting is not black or white. As a little experience is gained, it can be incorporated with exciting results. Sometimes you have to act on faith that the advice of friends or a doctor, or even something you read in a book, is valid and useful. As the toddler learns independence by walking in small steps and falling down frequently, so parenting is learned. Don't be afraid to take the first step. It is never too late.

Chapter 7

Parenting the School-age Child

"I really dreaded taking Glynnis to school. Somehow I felt that her teachers would judge me for being fat. I felt vulnerable and I resented the school, and probably undermined their working with Glynnis," says Marty, age 30, an adult child of an alcoholic who is a compulsive overeater.

Working with the School

Starting school is a traumatic time as it signifies entering a new phase of parenting. While most families have some problem in letting go, this is a greater problem for the family with alcoholism.

Entering partnerships is difficult for those affected by alcoholism for it requires two parenting skills which may be under-developed . . . *trust*, and the *ability to negotiate*.

Marty is typical: "All of my suspiciousness and compulsive worrying about life in general began to be focused on the school. Would Glynnis have the right teacher? Would they protect her if other kids picked on her? My fears also came out. Would they judge my fatness or my wife's thinness and see us as not fit parents?

"Her going to school brought up my childhood issues about school. All my childhood I dreaded my teachers finding out about my father's drinking. Was this why I was, in some ways, advertising our family's problems by being fat, to force her teachers to help her? Of course, I also worried if Glynnis was as bright as we thought she was? I obsessed over it all."

Grades K-3 —
Trust as the Basis of Partnership

Rule: Parents need to learn to trust the school.

Your attitude toward your child's school affects your child's adjustment to it (Morrow, Wilson, 1961). If you support the school, your child will learn how to transfer trust from one adult to another. If you question the teachers and principal and second-guess and undermine them, your children will be caught in the middle. They may begin to obsess about who to believe. You, their Mommy or Daddy, or should they believe their very nice teacher?

A major way that your attitude toward the school shows is in how you trust. Do you withdraw? Not get involved? Or are you over-involved? Trust is complicated. The school needs to be trusted to make the right decision for your child. This means learning to share power. It doesn't mean that you are not involved, you are, but you are giving up some control that you have had up till now as the only decision-maker for your child. Trust also means learning to trust your child's emerging ability to learn and to follow through. This requires letting them go as well.

The Impact of Addiction

Learning to trust is especially hard for the child who has grown up with a parent suffering from alcoholism, for it involves giving up control and being vulnerable (Black, 1981). Trust is also a major problem for the recovering person who is trying to do everything right (Wallace, 1985).

"That was me, particularly after the birth of my second child, Alicia, when I had a slip," sighs Maggie, 36, an adult child of an alcoholic and a alcoholic and prescription drug abuser who we met in Chapter 5. "I never thought I would, but having two children began to feel like two too many and I began to drink. Unfortunately, it was a public slip. I even went drunk to Tim's first parent-teacher conference. After that, I felt that I had to make up to Tim, and prove to the school that I was fit. I decided to prove it by controlling everything the school did to make sure they did it right. Eventually I learned to take my own inventory and not the school's. I owned my perfectionism as my problem."

The authors have found that parents who have been affected by alcoholism often approach the school in a guarded fashion. They will either want to take total control away from the school or relinquish all authority to the school. Those who have been affected by alcoholism fear that they will be judged. Often the school is seen as the ultimate parent. Since many of those who live with alcoholism know parents as punitive figures who can't be fully trusted, they expect the same from the school. This may lead them to either grossly over- or under-react to imagined or real events.

The answer to this dilemma is to begin to learn to trust, and what better opportunity than to start with the school? This doesn't mean suspending all your own thoughts about what is best for your child and blindly following the school's directions. It does mean entering into a partnership with the school where you don't doubt the sincerity of their motivation, but may at times question their decisions.

. . . The Acting-out Child

The behavior of the acting-out child is often intensified due to conflict between school and parents. The seeds of acting-out behavior in a child can be sown at any time. Such behavior can be a result of the mixed messages a child receives from parents and from teachers (Ginott, 1965). When a child is asked to divide loyalty or to choose a side, the child often opts instead *to act out his or her conflict by breaking the rules.* Their defiant behavior is designed to call attention to their pain, their fear concerning what they are being asked to do. It is almost as if the child is saying, "I'm going to make sure *you* will notice me and take care of me, because I can't do what you are expecting me to do."

Maggie speaks about her son Tim: "Tim began to have problems before I went back in an alcoholism treatment center. I really challenged the authority of the school and confused Tim. I recall one incident when he was learning multiplication. I taught him my way and when he said that the teacher was doing it another way, I told him the teacher was wrong. Shortly after this he began to be a behavior problem in school. It was almost as if he *couldn't* be good since I was telling him that in essence he had to choose between loyalty to the school or to me.

"The school was aware something was wrong and they asked me to come in for a conference. I did. Drunk. I felt that they were picking on Tim. I left in a huff. I drove there and took Tim home with me afterwards. I really wasn't safe to drive. The school called Gary at work and told him what had occurred. This led to a major blow-up, one of many, with Tim back in the middle, for 'his teacher had made Mommy and Daddy fight.' Poor Timmy, always taking responsiblity for the problems, always his mother's protector."

Once the school is brought into a partnership, and made aware of the reasons for at least some of the acting-out behavior, they can help in working with your child in school and evaluating your child to see if he or she needs professional help.

"We were lucky that when things calmed down at home, so did Tim. The school was very helpful in working with Tim once they understood what was going on at home. They were also able to give him support while I was away at the treatment center."

Forming the Partnership with the School

In working with the school, follow these guidelines:

1. *Get involved with school activities.* One way to learn to trust the school is to get to know it. Become involved in school-based activities. Volunteer for school events. You need not go to all, just enough so that you, your child and the school know that you care enough to be involved. School trips, bake sales, book sales and special events all provide opportunities for you to get to know the school personnel and policies. It is also an interesting way to get to know your child in a social setting. There is really no reason *not* to get involved. Take a personal day from work. After all, if your children aren't your personal concern, what is?

2. *Go to parent-teacher conferences.* These are opportunities you have to sit down with your child's teachers and consult with them and ask questions. You can also call a parent-teacher conference if you are concerned about a specific problem or your child's progress in general.

3. *Go over homework with your child.* It is important for your child's education that you support the school's efforts. While the school is the main academic educator, it can't do the job without you, the parents. As concerned parents, you should also know what your child is learning and how she or he feels about it.

4. *Join the parent-teacher organization.* Become an active partner with not only the school but also with other concerned parents. Your child's school needs your support.

5. *Support and encourage the school to address alcoholism and drug abuse.* You are now knowledgeable about how addiction affects families, children and parents. Work with your school to address these issues in the curriculum and among the faculty.

6. *Watch your own tendencies toward perfectionism and impulsivity.* Try not to act these out. Schools are run by people and they do make mistakes. If there is a problem, don't confront the administration first. Try to work it through. Remember you are a model for how your children will handle conflict.

Grades 4-6 —
Working with Your Child

Rule: Parents need to learn to monitor their child's school work.

Some parents find the task of working with their child on school work an enjoyable challenge. Others have difficulty, and it is often their children who have the most trouble with school. The task of teaching your children to manage homework is an important one. Learning how to pace themselves, when to do an assignment, what to do first, are important lessons not only for school but also for life. For example, children need to learn that they won't finish an assignment due on Monday if they start it a half-hour before bedtime on Sunday night. This is also not a good preparation for a child going to sleep, as the pressure of homework can leave a child unsettled and result in sleeplessness. Eventually when children and parents work together, a rhythm of school work can be developed.

The Impact of Addiction

Alcoholism affects children in numerous ways. Children who grow up in a home with a parent who is actively alcoholic often have to hunt for a safe place to do their homework.

A safe place to do homework is one which is quiet, which allows the child to concentrate and which has room to lay out and organize their papers and work. Frequently the home with active alcoholism is not conducive to study. This means an alternative place needs to be found. The non-alcoholic parent needs to encourage his or her child to not only find a study area, but also encourage the child to go there. Safe places can be a friend's, neighbor's or relative's home, a library, or after-school center. Sometimes if the school is made aware of the active disease at home, teachers can encourage your child to do some of their work during free times during the school day. Talk to your child's guidance counselor if there is active alcoholism at home. Trust the school to work with you on this.

... *The Perfectionistic Child*

The roots of perfectionism can be planted at any time in a child's life. Often perfectionism emerges when the child begins to receive homework. Homework is the first concrete series of tasks that the child receives from someone outside the family. Warning signs that perfectionism is present can be noted earlier in such actions as would elicit the description "perfect little miss," or "the perfect man of the house" of a four-year-old. This behavior does not frequently signal the alarm in a parent or in the school that a child's need for all 'A's can generate. And yet the cause for both behaviors can be the same, namely the child's need for perfection and for total control over his or her environment (Bandura, Walters, 1971).

When a child comes from a home with alcoholism, it is easy to speculate as to the cause of their need for perfection. Often it is simply the need to try to control all that is controllable in a chaotic home environment. Even adult children of alcoholics may create chaos around themselves. They have become so accustomed to chaos that they create it, however inadvertently, so that they have something around with which to organize their responses to the world. Their children, reared in a home organized around chaos, will learn to respond accordingly.

This was the case with Glynnis when she reached the fourth grade. It became apparent that the "perfect little miss" had some big problems.

"I blamed myself," Marty recalls. "Growing up in an alcoholic home, I vowed that I wouldn't marry anyone who drank. I didn't. I married someone who ate, and purged. I eat and eat. I'm just as addicted as an alcoholic, and our family life has been chaotic. At first I thought it was cute that Glynnis would be there to take care of me or to ask my wife Lisa if she should call the doctor after Lisa had just thrown up again. Now it doesn't seem so cute at all to watch her pull her hair out when she can't do a math problem correctly."

Relief came from an unexpected source. "The school turned out to be as worried as we were," Marty says, pleased that his trust was rewarded. "They had Glynnis seen by the school psychologist. She suggested we go to the Child Guidance Clinic for family counseling. It's helping."

Homework Guidelines

Since homework can be a troublesome area, the following are guidelines that the authors have found useful.

1. *Do homework at a set time each day.* Have a regular time of day when your child is expected to do homework. This may be directly after school before they go out to play or right after dinner. You can experiment with what time works best for your child. Each child has his or her own needs. Some need to blow off energy after a day of sitting still in school. Others need to build on the structure of the school day to enable them to focus on their schoolwork before they play. Get to know your children individually so you can encourage them to do whatever is best. Teach your children to be consistent in their approach.

2. *Go over your child's homework.* Find out who is the better parent to either go over the homework or to go over a particular subject. Share your expertise, whether it's in math, English, history or some other subject.

3. *Praise your child's work.* There will be mistakes. This is normal. Don't be an overly critical parent. Find something great in what your child has done — their persistence, penmanship, attitude, creativity or courage in tackling a different subject. Reward children by praising them for mastering a thorny problem, or for trying and not giving up.

4. *Homework problems should be reported to the teacher.* If your child doesn't bring home school work but his peers do, the teacher should be informed that somehow your child is not getting the message that there is work that needs to be done at home. Or if your child is having continued problems with mastering an aspect of mathematics or English, the teacher should be consulted.

5. *If problems persist, request a consultation* with the teacher, then the guidance counselor. Your child may need a special approach to learning which may only be determined by doing evaluation testing.

6. *Spend quality time with your child.* Don't let the doing of homework be the only time you sit down together. This will only encourage your child to develop more problems with his or her homework in order to keep you involved with them.

Developing Rules for Children

It is important for children to have consistent rules. From consistent rules the child learns how to make choices and to deal with consequences. It is normal for children to test rules. It is also normal for children to test what is the truth. They test this by not only inventing a truth or two but also by watching other children and adults around them and catching them in either not following the rules, or in not being truthful. This is how a child learns (Ginott, 1965).

Consistency is not the hallmark of the home with active addictions, such as alcoholism. From inconsistent rules the child will learn either rigidity, as seen in the perfectionistic child, or that rules do not count, as demonstrated by the acting-out child. Inconsistent rule-setting, as seen in a parent punishing a behavior when drunk, and rewarding the same behavior when sober, often puts pressure on a child to develop their own rules.

. . . The Case of Black or White

Surprisingly, when children make their own rules, they are always more punitive and more strict than an adult would be. Since they have little life experience to guide them, and since it is normal for a child to try to please, they try to fit their acts into one of two boxes — black or white, right or wrong. Without adult modeling and guidance these two boxes can become their only frame of reference. As they mature they will have difficulty in defining gray. The result can be a series of failures as the child tries but can never quite live up to being right all of the time. To deal with this, the child may withdraw, or act out.

Gray is a color learned later in life for everyone. Those affected by alcoholism may have even greater difficulty in learning this.

"I don't feel I learned gray, until maybe recently. Perhaps this is why I've been so punitive with Tim. I saw his behavior as totally wrong since he wasn't doing what I wanted him to do," states Maggie.

Rule-Making

It is difficult for parents to develop rules objectively for their children when they have had little experience with consistent rules in their own childhood. You should remember that children need to be taught to obey. This experience can be positive if the child's individual temperament is understood. That is, are they easily frustrated, afraid to try, in need of a great deal of praise, likely to cover failure with anger or likely to display other reactions? Remember, a child will be frustrated. This is part of learning and accompanies all learning. To help you along, consider the following suggested guidelines. Do not rush. Take these one at a time.

1. *Have regular family meetings.* Regular meetings of a family provide a way for the family to come together, plan, air concerns and settle problems. In such meetings everyone gets a vote and everyone gets a say, no matter how young.

2. *Develop rules by sitting down with your children and discussing them.* At family meetings have each child contribute ideas about what needs to be done, and who would be best to do it. You and your spouse need to make sure that children do not over-commit themselves, or commit to doing things that they are not yet developmentally able to do.

3. *Post rules on the refrigerator.* Everyone goes in the refrigerator. As such it can be a focal point for family activity. Post the rules there with a daily check-list. This way you can just note if the garbage has been taken out, you don't need to preach about it. Use stars or smiling face stickers to mark a job well done, or a good week.

4. *Set total, not partial limits.* If you tell your child that he can splash his younger sister as long as he does not get her wet, you will have guaranteed yourself a deluge of trouble. Limits should be clear and understandable. Have clear rewards and clear consequences. Negotiate this ahead of time, particularly if there have been problems with one or more of your children following through. Rewards can be given for 70 to 80 percent compliance, with bonuses for 90 to 100 percent. Discuss this with your spouse and children and see what is best. Remember, rewards can be a half-hour more of TV on Friday night or an extra scoop of ice cream. They should never be anything that will break the family's bankroll or compromise other family activities.

5. *Don't accept excuses.* This only teaches lying and the art of excuse-making. If a rule is made, it should be followed. No excuses.

6. *Work instead to either negotiate the rule or to help your child comply with it.* For example, if the rule is to be home at 6 p.m. for dinner and your child is late, ask him if he remembers the rule. Make sure your children know how to tell time. See if they need a watch. Try to understand if the problem is peer pressure not to leave a game. Work on these issues instead of accepting an excuse which will only teach your child to be a better excuse-maker.

7. *Have allowances.* There is pro and con as to whether allowances should be tied to family chores. Some experts feel that if children see that their contribution is needed within the family, that this is all the reward that they require; that they need not and should not be paid for doing a chore needed by the family. Allowances are not earned, but rather are a division of the family earnings so that each person may take care of personal needs. Other experts feel that an allowance should be earned and tied to chores. There is no right or wrong. Again, this is an issue to be discussed with your spouse and with your children.

If the rules aren't working, ask yourself:
● Are you making too many demands at once on your child?
● Are you expecting more than your child at this age and under these circumstances can do?
● Is the discipline understood?
● Are you trying to gain compliance by force, bullying or bribing?
● Do directions have too many explanations, making them unclear?
● Do you both agree with what is required of your child?
● Are you keeping the child's individual temperament in mind in planning your approach?

Rule: Parents need to monitor and not over-schedule their children's activities.

As parents you want the best for your child. This often means that you are more than willing to assist your child in pursuing any latent or manifest talents. For the child who has many talents or interests, the result can be increased stress as the child runs from the school to piano, ballet, voice, karate, swimming, track, all scheduled and chauffeured by the parent.

The Impact of Addiction

Compulsive *over-scheduling* is more frequently found in the recovering home. The reason for this is that families with active addiction often have difficulty being as organized as this amount of scheduling requires. Before we discuss the downside of this over-scheduling, the gains should be understood. Scheduled activities are important for children need child-centered activities and a child-centered home.

The reason for the frequency of over-scheduling in the recovering home is two-fold. First, the family may be trying to make up for lost time. In some families this occurs because in the active phase of alcoholism the children were deprived of positive parental attention and now in recovery, time is taken to make this up to them. Also some recovering families tend to over-schedule their children to compensate for the guilt they feel for not being home when they need to go to meetings.

They get caught in a time squeeze, as Maggie illustrates: "After I left the alcoholism treatment center, I really needed to go to meetings but I felt bad that I wasn't home for Tim. Tim also got on my nerves. It was easier to get him involved in Little League, karate and the Cub Scouts than to spend quality time with him. And so I did."

In adult children of alcoholics, the lost time phenomenon is experienced as the loss of part of childhood: lost opportunities, lost time to pursue their interests, to play.

"As a parent, I've tried to undo what my parents 'did' to me. I wanted to give my children every opportunity to explore their interests," says Marty, a proud father and the adult child of an alcoholic.

The Perfectionistic Child Revisited

Over-scheduling can inadvertently send your children the message that they need to perform and excel in all that you are "encouraging" them to do. This can burden a perfectionistic child, who is still trying to please a parent, into feeling that he or she has to master all of these new activities.

"Unfortunately, Glynnis has to be perfect in all she does. Our therapist tells us that our expectations are too high. Glynnis tries to develop her interests but becomes increasingly frustrated when she isn't perfect on the third try. Somehow this must be coming from us — Lisa and I," complains Marty anxiously.

Guidelines for Scheduling

Since scheduling is difficult, even for adults, here are four guidelines that may make the task easier. Add to them as you find other strategies that work.

1. *Practice is important.* Often children become disappointed and frustrated when they cannot perform a new skill well. Children need to be encouraged and rewarded, not punished or threatened into practicing. Practicing a half-hour a day, whether at a sport or a musical instrument, could be an expectation that is discussed and posted on the refrigerator. Children also need to be encouraged to build on small steps, not to expect mastery after only a couple of

trials. Expectations which are too high are a major reason why children drop out of activities.

2. *Losing interest is OK.* If children learn that they can withdraw from an activity without undue parental pressure, it makes it easier for them to commit to another. This is one way they can learn their limits, and their interests.

3. *Children need to be paced.* They should try one skill area at a time. Once there is some success at one, another can be added and then its impact evaluated.

4. *Children need free time.* They should not be over-scheduled. Over-scheduling only creates additional pressure on children to not only perform, but puts pressure on them to juggle their schedules to get to the various activities. This is unhealthy. Childen learn a great deal from free play time, this needs to be part of how they spend their time, too.

Rule: Parents need to be aware of who their children choose as friends.

Children are begining to form friendships. They are becoming independent and are choosing who they want to be their friends. Bonds are formed between friends and socializing begins to take place away from parental supervision. Children at this age are establishing culturally appropriate sex roles. To this end, most of the friends your child will initially choose will be of the same sex. With these friends they will experiment with the different aspects of what their family and the greater society expect from them (Simmons, Rosenberg, 1975; Hill, Lynch, 1983).

School-age childen also have a high level of fantasy which they will tend to act out. Risk-taking becomes more common as children develop their skills, independence and have the means to experiment on a larger scale with their fantasies. As cognitive abilities are developing, there is greater learning which can lead to more creative play (Lewis, Lewis, 1984). Parental guidance is required but becomes more difficult as children become more independent and more ambivalent about direct parental involvement.

The Impact of Addiction

In homes with active alcoholism and other active addictions, children do not often receive the encouragement they need to develop friendships. From socializing, a child develops a sense of self. Many children of alcoholics have a hard time making friends, which is another deprivation. When having friends is interfered with, the child is delayed in developing not only a sense of self, but also in learning what to expect from others (Simmons, Rosenburg, 1975).

. . . Compulsive Dependency and Friendships

"I wasn't able to bring friends home, so I stopped having any friends," says Maggie, a recovering alcoholic and ACoA. "Of course I had acquaintances. I responded to what I thought they thought about me. I walked around embarrassed, withdrawn, for I felt others 'knew' my family secret. I was so locked into how *they* felt that I never examined how *I* felt. They were more important than I was. My imagined opinion of what they thought was more valid than my own. I was dependent on them, but not close to them, for I really didn't know them. I learned dependency and distance from my friends. Now my dependence and distance is present in my marriage and with my children."

. . . Acting Out

Children learn from their parents and the same dynamics, here dependence and distance, can be learned and manifested in a different manner by a different child.

"I think Tim feels the same way," Maggie notes. "I've now had more than one slip. Every time I do, it seems Tim gets into more trouble in school. He is so angry. He has friends but now that he is eleven, I worry what they are doing. I fear that he's using something. He needs to be with his friends, but if all they are doing is getting high, I wonder how close they can be? I also wonder if all his behavior in school isn't designed to keep his teachers involved but not too close."

Supervising Friendships

1. *Let your child choose his or her friends.* But get to *know them.* Have them to your home. Meet them. Talk to them.
2. *Get to know their parents.* This will be helpful in following up on where your children are and what they are doing. It also may be enjoyable for you to support your child's friendships by getting acquainted with their friend's parents, and doing some family activities together.

3. *Know where your children are.* It is important to know their activities. Drug and alcohol use is not uncommon in the upper elementary school grades.

Summary

When children enter school there are suddenly many more variables to deal with. Parents need to learn to work in partnership with the school, which means learning to negotiate with the school. This raises issues of trust and vulnerability for those who have been affected by addiction. Aside from working with the school, parents face new challenges, for children as they get older have different needs. Children require an active involvement from their parents in a variety of new activities, which range from support in doing their homework to supervision of going to a friend's home or planning free-time activities. Active parenting means learning to be supportive and learning to let go and not be compulsive in your worrying, control or scheduling of your child's life and time.

Chapter 8

Parenting Adolescents

"Tim is quite a handful at 15. He's reached puberty, discovered girls and I think he's using something. He's so different from Alicia. You'd hardly know that she's there. Tim has always made his presence felt," observes Maggie, now 43, an adult child of an alcoholic, and an alcoholic.

Puberty and Early Adolescence — Ages 12 to 15

Adolescence is a time of major transition between childhood and adulthood, when children change from being just children into looking and acting, at least at times, more like adults. For all their drama, adolescents are covering up dealing with their fear of the massive physical changes going on within their bodies and the major social changes going on in their lives.

Adolescence is a difficult time for the adolescents, for they are both frightened and excited. This results in their being moody, angry, self-righteous, always right, yet vulnerable, for they are so obviously striving to become independent, and to find out who they are and what they need. To accomplish the developmental task of becoming independent, the adolescent will need to develop new coping methods and new support systems outside of the family. Like any change, these new coping methods, new friends, new ways of handling conflict and hurt, will take practice in order for your teenage children to decide that what is working, what should be kept as part of their new style and what needs to be replaced. In the meantime, these changes often result in an increase in the amount of tension and potential conflict within their families.

Change is difficult. As with any period of change, expectations are in flux in the family with the adolescent. This is why adolescence is also a period of conflict between parent and child. Previous predictable patterns of family interactions are altered. Parents often alternately expect too much or too little from their children. The shifting ground causes the children to either feel like they "are being treated like a baby" or that too much is expected from them. Adolescents and their parents often react to these changes by displaying a remarkable ability to lock horns.

Parents find adolescence difficult because they need to give up the protection which they have up to now afforded their children. Allowing their children to go out into the world knowing they will be hurt is not easy. Seeing their children in pain and not being able to reach them often incites even the calmest parents to lose control.

Adolescents caught in their conflict of wanting to be protected and at the same time needing to prove their independence, often are pushed by their parents' increased demands and lack of calm into displaying a new level of apathy, even in previously good parent-child relationships. Yet for all the problems that occur during this period, for most adolescents this tranformation into an independent adult cannot happen quickly enough. And for most parents it occurs too rapidly.

Rule: Parents need to separate their own adolescence from what their adolescents are experiencing.

Memories of your own adolescence are sure to engender strong feelings. Often if you cannot recall memories before adolescence, you can remember at least part of your teenage years. The tasks of adolescence such as separation from family and making one's own identity are very complex and for many adults not fully completed. As a result, the intense feelings that accompanied these issues, such as anger at authority, are often near the surface. This is why some adults have trouble realizing that they are no longer adolescents, and that life for their children holds more options — opportunities as well as dangers — that it did when they were in their teens.

Yet your memories of your own adolescence, however painful they may be, can help you understand your adolescent child. Besides allowing you to empathize with the turmoil your child is experiencing, clear recall may also help you predict what their next potential crisis will be. In recalling your own attempts to deal with such problems as being rebuffed by the girl of your dreams, or not having big breasts when every other girl did, you can help guide your children through these extraordinarily painful, yet normal, events of adolescence.

The Impact of Addiction

Being able to separate your own experiences from your teenage child's is difficult enough, but if you are still emotionally dealing with the struggles of your own adolescence, it becomes a real challenge. This is frequently the situation facing the recovering parent. Many people who develop alcoholism began drinking in their teens. From the point at which they approached dependence on alcohol they also stopped growing emotionally (Strauss, 1976). This makes raising a child more difficult, as developmentally the parent in early recovery may be resolving issues still left over from their own adolescence.

For the adult child of an alcoholic, growth may have been stunted even earlier (O'Gorman, 1975). Parenting a child who is ahead of you developmentally is more than a little difficult. Separating yourself and helping your teenage child go through something that you have not completed yourself can raise the anxiety level for both parent and child. Children can become more anxious if they feel they are carrying the burden of unraveling the dilemma of adolescence for both of you. They may decide that you are no better at dealing with their problems than they are, leading to either discounting you or feeling a need to rescue you. You can become even more anxious because of your fear of your perceived and real limitations. It does not feel good to fail your children.

The Need for Alateen

What can you do? As someone who has been affected by the alcoholism of a parent or a spouse, you have many resources at your disposal. One of the most useful is Alateen. Alateen is a self-help recovery program for young people who have been affected by alcoholism. It is sponsored by Al-Anon and open to teens regardless of who the alcoholic in their life is — you, a grandparent, uncle or even a close family friend. Alateen is peer support and peer learning at its best.

Tim, the oldest child of Maggie and Gary, is someone who could have benefited from Alateen earlier if he had been encouraged to attend meetings. It was only when his parents forced him to deal with his own drug use, as we shall see, that they also strongly encouraged him to get some support and understanding for what it was like to live with two adult children of alcoholics, one of whom was also an alcoholic.

Encouraging your children to go to Alateen is very important because not only do they *learn* about how alcoholism affected them, they also learn to take *responsibility* for their thoughts and actions. By encouraging attendance at Alateen, you are also encouraging your child to learn to be independent (O'Gorman, 1984).

There are also many secondary benefits. By having members share their feelings, Alateen breaks down the isolation that your child may be experiencing and teaches him or her to interact in a positive, structured, peer-learning experience. Although there is an adult sponsor from Al-Anon at the meeting, the chair-personship rotates between the teenage members. As a result, adolescents also learn other important skills: how to lead a meeting, share feelings and maybe most importantly, how to trust.

You Need To Be a Parent, Not a Peer

Unfortunately, some parents deal with the problem of being developmentally in a similar position as their child by identifying too closely with the child. They take vicarious, and perhaps unconscious, pleasure in their adolescent's acting out, with the result of spurring them on. They enjoy the attention their adolescent receives, and incite their teenager to get more. They excuse the more excessive behavior as "sowing wild oats" and foster the development of greater excesses. They see all that their teenager does as a reflection on their own desirability. They have not been able to see their teenager as a separate person. Such parents are not parenting their teenager, but merely being a peer to their child. This leaves in question the issue of who will parent a child if their parent cannot. The answer today is often the adolescent's peer group.

. . . Compulsive Dependency

The Case of Eating Disorders

Being a peer instead of a parent can have other effects in the family touched by alcoholism and/or addictions. Eating disorders can result from a parent and a child being too *dependent* on each other. Family dynamics often provide the breeding ground for the development of food-related compulsive dependencies — bulimia, anorexia nervosa and overeating. Eating disorders are more typically found in families in which there is a pressure to be thin, a specialness concerning food, isolation, poor conflict resolution, rigidity and over-protectiveness (Striegel-Moore, Silberstein, Rodin, 1986). These families appear much like a family with alcoholism, organized around food instead of alcohol. This may account for the greater prevalence of eating disorders in adult children of alcoholics reported by a growing number of clinicians (Jonas, 1986).

These family dynamics are compounded by society. For families which have not been able to model control, either of food or alcohol use, society offers a simple method to the adolescent who wants to appear to be in control, and this is dieting. Dieting or purging can easily dovetail with the adolescent's desire to prove her maturity, control and independence from her family, particularly if she sees her family as out of control (Steele, 1980). Proving their own control by dieting or purging can be one way for adolescents to separate from their family and is seen by many adolescents who do this as positive.

Extreme dieting can also be a sign that the *pressure* of adolescence is too great and reflects a desire to return to a pre-pubertal look, maintaining oneself as a child in the eyes of society (Selvini-Palazzoli, 1978). For the child of the alcoholic this issue becomes even more complex. One is forced to ponder if the adolescent who is dieting or purging may perhaps be wishing to return to a less complex time, or a safer time, when they did not have to deal with their awakening sexuality.

Why would anyone do this to themself? The reason is that personal dissatisfaction with one part of a child's functioning can lead to an overall devaluation of him or herself (Harter, 1985). The child diets and purges based on positive motivation, to feel *in control* and to improve her image of herself.

Although eating disorders occur more commonly among women, Glynnis is the daughter of two adult children of alcoholics, both of whom have eating disorders. Glynnis emulated the behavior of both parents, both of whom prized thinness, and developed an eating disorder.

From the time she was a child Glynnis was concerned about her mother's and father's health. She was aware that her mother's purging was not normal, and she would ask if she could call the doctor. She was equally obsessed with her father's being overweight. She became a perfectionistic, parental child who was very dependent on her parents, especially her mother. Family therapy when she was in grade school addressed her obsessive, perfectionistic habits, but not her dependency. As an adolescent she continued to be dependent on her mother, and also to be her mother's main caretaker.

When she reached puberty, Glynnis became alarmed with the normal increase in body fat that accompanies this growth. Her insecurity led her to become increasingly sensitive to what she perceived as social demands and appropriate sex-role behavior. She longed for the prepubescent body which is held in such high esteem in the teen fashion world. She feared that she would not be popular now that she was "fat." She felt out of control. For all these reasons she began to diet and to do what she saw her mother doing. She began to purge herself of food.

Glynnis wanted to improve her self-esteem. She was trying not to devalue herself so she tried to take care of her problem in the very best way she could. She was overly dependent on her mother and very loyal to her family traditions. She did what would be expected in this situation. When Lisa saw what was happening to her daughter, it was too much for her:

"It was like looking in the mirror for the first time. I couldn't believe what I saw."

Overeaters Anonymous

Parenting requires *conscious effort*. Lisa shows how purposeful a parent may need to be.

"I realized that I couldn't live through Glynnis anymore. I began to work my Al-Anon and Overeaters Anonymous programs, and practiced detaching with love. Eventually it worked, but it was so difficult.

"I used, or manipulated, if you will, the fact that Glynnis was very dependent on me and invited her to go to Overeaters Anonymous meetings with me. I also worked my program and began not to purge. Glynnis began to change her eating behavior as well. It was scary when I realized just how much power I really had over her."

Sexual Feelings

Rule: Parents need to accept their children as having sexual feelings.

Many teachers have commented that the worst grade to teach is the seventh grade. Everyone is in some phase of puberty and they all want to touch each other but don't know how. So they punch, slap and take things from each other all day long.

Sexual feelings begin to stir prior to puberty. Girls and boys begin to notice each other. They begin to take greater interest in their appearance. They become flirtatious. And then they begin to change physically. The age at which puberty occurs varies between boys and girls, with girls tending to mature earlier. The actual age of the onset of puberty is coming down, meaning that for some precocious children early adolescence does not begin in junior high school but in elementary school (Bell, 1980).

Whenever puberty occurs, parents find it difficult to accept that their children are having sexual feelings. The greater *fear* is that since children have these feelings, they will *act* on them. This brings with it the fear of pregnancy, the fear of sexually transmitted diseases and the fear that their children will fall in love and be hurt. There may also be moral considerations. In some ways dealing with their children's emerging sexuality is the most difficult problem that parents face.

And there is reason for concern. Adolescents are becoming sexually more active at younger ages. By age 15, 23 percent of girls are no longer virgins. By 18, this figure jumps to 57 percent. But all this sexual activity has not brought with it much pleasure. By 1982 there were over one million estimated unintended pregnancies in the United States. And one in three sexually active teenagers feel so guilty and frightened that they can be described as "unhappy nonvirgins" (Kolodny, Bratter, Deep, 1984).

The Impact of Addiction

Alcoholism loosens emotional boundaries within families, which can lead to an increase in the level of sexual tension (Steinglass, 1980). In some families this can foster a type of intense emotional closeness where children bond with a parent and begin to parent their parent. In the process, they may reject the efforts made by the same sex parent to care for the opposite-sex parent. They see their same sex parent as a failure in taking care of the needs of their opposite-sex parent. They feel that only they can step into the breach. And they do it with all their innocence.

Intoxication can create *confusion* as to who is who within a family. It is not uncommon for a father who is intoxicated to call his daughter by his wife's name, or to even think that his daughter is his wife. This can lead to inappropriate touching, fondling, name-calling and even physical acts. The potential for sexual closeness between parent and child is not limited to the drinking parent. The child's need to comfort the non-alcoholic parent by such activities as getting into bed with their parent when the alcoholic parent is out of the home can lead to the same type of inappropriate activity. Sadly, incest occurs with much greater frequency in alcoholic homes (Black, 1985).

It is no wonder that those affected by alcoholism have difficulty in dealing with the sexuality of their children. For to deal successfully with these issues means to have resolved the problems from their own childhood. Doing this while parenting an adolescent means resolving these issues under great pressure.

Lisa, an ACoA, recalls some of her adolescent memories: "I remember that when I was a teenager, I had to be careful what I wore, for my father would stare at my body. For example, I would never walk around in a nightgown. I always wore a bathrobe, no matter what the temperature was. I was most afraid when he was drunk that he would do something. So it's hard for me to see Glynnis just reaching puberty walking around in front of Marty. I feel I need to protect her. I know it's crazy; Marty would never do anything but my fear is still there."

It is important for these childhood issues to be dealt with. If there was any incest or fear of incest in your family of origin, you will need psychotherapy along with, not in lieu of your 12-step program, to help you resolve this. And these issues can be resolved if you pick a good therapist and work with him or her, and use your program (see Chapter 11). Remember, as difficult as these problems are to confront, it is better to resolve them within yourself than to carry them on for another generation.

Later Adolescence — Ages 15 to 19

Rule: Parents need to talk to their children about alcohol and drug usage and intervene early with even suspected alcohol or drug abuse.

Experimentation with alcohol and drugs begins for many children in junior high school. Like the sexual experimentation which it often accompanies, the use of mood-altering substances is often hidden from parents. Parents may only begin to realize there is a problem when the adolescent is older. Unfortunately by then the signs of a developing problem are often too difficult to miss (Finn, O'Gorman, 1981).

Drug and Alcohol Use

— Guilt . . . Guilt . . . Guilt

Guilt is a strongly felt emotion not only for the alcoholic but also for other family members (Wallace, 1985). What stops many families with alcoholism and/or other addictions from dealing with the alcohol or drug usage of their child is often their own guilt. This guilt can be paralyzing and result in denial until the evidence is overwhelming. Guilt can also inadvertently precipitate alcohol or drug usage in an adolescent. Or guilt can stop parents from talking to their children, leaving them to struggle with their peers' use of alcohol and drugs.

Maggie has known since Tim was about 11 that he was using drugs.

"I knew but I didn't want to know. I was so wrapped up in my own guilt that alcoholism was happening in yet another generation, and that I hadn't been able to stop it, that I just couldn't deal with Tim. I devoted myself to my own recovery, hoping that somehow this would help Tim. Of course it would have helped if I spoke to him but I was immobilized and I couldn't. Dealing with him began to feel like a distraction from what I needed to do for myself, so I didn't deal with him. I was so guilty, and feeling so sorry for myself, that I began drinking and using Valium again.

"It was only when Tim announced that he was going to drop out of high school that I realized I had to get involved. Gary and I knew the reason, and it was drugs. When we finally confronted Tim, I knew why we had avoided it for so long. He told us, 'You have your drugs —booze — and I have mine. What's the big deal?' He was trying to tell us that since he didn't have *our* problem, he didn't have *a* problem. Gary and I were both so guilty. As adult children of alcoholics we felt that maybe he was right and it was our fault. We both felt that we had done this to Tim."

Gary illustrates the problem from the point of view of the spouse who is also the adult child of an alcoholic and compulsive gambler.

"I've always been very supportive to Maggie once she began the battle with booze and pills. I know it was tough, her slips (back into using alcohol). But I vowed I wouldn't leave her as other husbands have done to the alcoholic wives. I guess you can say I'm loyal, one of my better traits.

"When Tim became so obviously ill, I realized that I had to take some firm action. I just couldn't focus on Maggie to the exclusion of the kids. Her drinking, at the point that Tim became ill, made me feel that I had to choose between them. I did. I put energy into Tim, maybe for the first time in his life. Maggie, no longer the sole focus of my attention, actually began going back to A.A. I went to more Al-Anon meetings. Together Maggie and I confronted Tim."

. . . Leading to Taking on Responsibility that Belongs to Your Child

Families in recovery can take on *too much* responsibility for the drug and alcohol problems of their children (Wallace, 1985). The fact that this is done out of love does not really help the child. When a family takes on too much responsibility, they deny their child the opporunity of confronting his own behavior. This only delays their child's dealing with his problem and may actually increase the likelihood of usage. This is what happened to Tim.

Says Maggie, "Gary and I were so guilty that we had to deal with it. So we took care of ourselves, and our guilt, first. I had a slip. We eventually got around to trying to figure out what to do with Tim.

"By then the message Tim had was that he wasn't to blame for his actions. So he blamed us, and we initially took the blame. We couldn't do anything right at that point. Thank God, we just took him and ourselves to an addiction treatment center, and I started A.A. We stopped trying to take care of Tim in isolation."

. . . Leading to Inadvertently Encouraging Use

Maggie illustrates another reaction of some recovering families to the alcohol or drug usage of their children.

"At least I'm not as bad as some parents I meet in A.A. At the first sign of any usage they cart their kids off to a meeting. I think that meetings must be the only time that they spend with their children. I know kids drink early but a 12-year-old at A.A. because he had a couple of beers? Come on!

"I wonder if some of these parents don't in some ways encourage their kids to use so that they can do their things, go to meetings together. These parents' philosophy seem to be: 'If you can't talk to your kid, have them drink, for you can talk to an alcoholic.' I don't think that philosophy helps anyone."

. . . Resulting in an Inability to Talk to Their Child about Alcohol and Drug Use

You don't need to be addicted to talk to your child about alcohol and drugs. You *do* need to do some homework. Consider your values, your behaviors, your personal and family history, your recreational patterns and entertaining practices. Once you have had an honest talk with yourself and your spouse, then you are ready to risk speaking to your child.

. . . The Child of the Alcoholic's View of Alcohol and Drug Use

Children of alcoholics often have an extreme reaction to the alcohol and drug usage of their peers. The authors have typically found young CoA's reactions to fall into one of three categories.

1. *Some will find peers who are experimenting early and they will join them.* So great is their fear that they will also develop a problem with alcohol that they can't wait to find out what will happen to them and so they start using early. If they do not immediately develop the problems with alcohol use that they see in their parents, they feel they are home free. Or course, they will not immediately develop the same problems with alcohol their parents have. That takes time. But they can develop alcohol problems that adolescents have. Unless there is someone present in their lives who understands this difference, adolescent children of alcoholics will feel that they have escaped developing alcoholism.

2. *Others will use drugs, but not alcohol.* Like Tim, they rationalize this as having their personal drug of choice. This is felt as understandable and justified as long as they do not use alcohol, since alcohol has demonstrated negative side-effects.

3. *Still other adolescents will refrain from any alcohol and drug usage.* They will also have immediate negative reactions to their peers and friends who use alcohol and drugs. They will experience feelings of betrayal, anger and possible depression over their friends' use. They may experiment with alcohol or drug usage but it will be much later than their peer group when they are older and surer of themselves.

Enlightened parents realize that their child's feelings about alcohol and drug usage is, in part, a reaction to unresolved family issues. While this is important to note, it is even more important to break through the conspiracy of silence that can exist within a family and *begin a dialogue* with your child about alcohol and drug abuse.

This does not mean just telling them your story. It means getting to know your child and letting him know his family history (who else in the family has a drug or alcohol problem) and its impact on their lives and that of their children. To have this conversation requires asking your children and wanting to know what they are doing, what their friends are doing. It also means finding out how they feel. Of course, you can't sit down, have one conversation, and acquit yourself. This has to be part of an ongoing dialogue, not a preachalogue or drunkalogue.

To Drink or Not?

The safest message to send your children about alcohol use is not to *drink* if alcoholism and/or addictions run in the family. By not drinking, your children will cut the risk of developing alcoholism to zero. This is also the most difficult message for most children to hear and accept.

Many adolescents experiment with alcohol for a variety of reasons: because they have seen their parents and other relatives drink, because their peers drink and because they see a lack of negative consequences in the way alcohol use is glamourized in the media. Adolescents feel immortal. If they see a movie or television star engage in high-speed driving after drinking, it only serves to support the notion that people can drink without experiencing problems. Inconsistent laws, such as those which permit the selling of drug paraphernalia, yet punish those who use drugs, compound the problem. Young people are quick to seize upon hypocrisy and will use it to defend drug use. For the same reason many young people do not take seriously the laws against purchasing alcohol and drinking and driving because of the way these laws are inconsistently enforced. Finally, young people, and some medical practitioners, do not believe that children can develop alcoholism. This is not true. Young people do develop alcoholism, and children of alcoholics are the single most at-risk group (O'Gorman, Lacks, 1979).

This is why it is important that you are clear what to expect from your children in their use of alcohol and drugs. This requires that you and your spouse make family rules and enforce them consistently. Doing that requires parents to face the controversial issue of whether those affected by alcoholism should drink.

Is alcohol use OK? Is drug use OK? Should it be discontinued if there are problems? What constitutes a problem? How will you and your child know if there is a problem? If it's not OK to drink or use drugs, children need to know why. And if it is OK, under what circumstances?

Some parents hesitate to deal with these issues, fearing that they will over-react. What to do?

First, realize that your decisions about alcohol or drug use are based on your experiences and on your family's values and behaviors. Second, understand that a behavior for you may have one meaning and the same behavior for your child may have another very different meaning.

For example, if wine is used in your family and is given to children, even in a diluted form to drink at Passover or Christmas, your child may well consider himself to be a drinker. In this society, the ritual and specialness of the wine may be overshadowed in your children's eyes by the fact that they have had a drink. It is important to clarify for your child under which circumstance alcohol is used or not used in your family, by who, and why.

If alcohol is not used by either you or your spouse, children should know why, and why you do not think that *they* should drink. If you do not drink alcohol because you are an alcoholic but your spouse does use alcohol, clarify the reasons to your child. Remember, your children will be watching you and waiting to know why you do what you do. They will also learn by imitating you.

Know the Law

Another consideration for parents on the issue of the alcohol and drug use of their children is the need for them to understand the legal age of purchase of alcohol, and the legal implications of drug use. Laws vary in each state. In many states laws not only forbid a child under age to buy alcohol but also holds servers in social settings liable for actions of minors under the influence. This means you if you serve your daughter's boyfriend, or if you allow your daughter to serve him. So along with the issue of family values is also the concern over the law.

There is obviously much to consider in deciding this question. So take your time and consider it. If you are still confused, see what guidance your child's school can offer. Get more information from groups with a variety of viewpoints. *The Federation of Parents for Drug Free Youth, Tough Love* and *Families in Action* are three excellent resources.

What To Do?

Be an *alert* parent and watch for the signs of alcohol or drug usage. If your child or any of their friends are showing any of the following signs, get involved, talk to your children and find out if they or their friends are using. If his or her friends are using, it will just be a matter of time before your child becomes curious and will experiment as well.

Signs of Alcohol and Drug Usage in Adolescents

1. *Health*
   a. Frequent excessive coughing
   b. Frequent infections
   c. Frequent small burns
   d. Weight loss, decreased appetite
   e. Weight gain, need for munchies
   f. Frequent headaches
   g. Cessation of menstruation
   h. Hyperactivity
   i. Illness in the morning, throwing up, lethargy, headaches

2. *Physical*
   a. Blood-shot eyes
   b. Runny nose, irritated nose
   c. Smell of marijuana or alcohol on clothing, or on breath
   d. Discoloration of skin, brownish-yellowish on forefinger and thumb
   e. Needle marks on arms, legs
   f. Accidents of any kind
   g. Dilated pupils

3. *Social and Emotional*
   a. Change in friends to those who are known users
   b. Concern of boyfriend or girlfriend regarding use
   c. Drop in grades
   d. Slurred, slow speech
   e. Inability to think clearly
   f. Diminished alertness
   g. Excessive sleeping, decrease in energy
   h. Unusual mood changes, depression, wide mood swings
   i. Increase in anxiety
   j. Hallucinations or paranoia
   k. Increase in secrecy
   l. Constant need for money
   m. Abundance of money from unexplained sources

If your child or his friends is displaying these symptoms, talk to them about it. Your family physician, trained clergyman, mental health professional or drug or alcohol rehabilitation professional should be consulted about your next step.

The Need for Independence

Rule: Parents need to encourage independence in their adolescents.

The main task of adolescence is *separation* and *individuation* from the family (Erikson, 1963) also called growing up. The close attachment that adolescents form with their peer groups is important in completing this task. Friends of your child actually assist your child in learning to rely less on you, the family. Peer groups also provide other services. For example, peers provide a place to obtain information. Peers are often the first people who an adolescent will go with a problem. Peers provide support. Whatever advice is given by peers is usually considered very carefully. Peers become the new experts in resolving life's issues, and parents are gradually seen as not as informed or as sensitive as friends. Peers also provide a place to socialize and activities which teach independent social skills.

This reliance on peers can belie the fact that the adolescent is highly ambivalent about becoming an adult. To achieve independence, adolescents require considerable support from their family in order to make the shift to relying more on their friends. *Parents need to guide* their children in determining who is a friend and why. Parents need to supervise what occurs with friends. Parents need to be available with support for their children through this sorting-out phase of what they need from friends and what they are willing to give in return. And, most importantly, parents need to remember the friendships made during adolescence are subject to rapid and painful changes.

The Impact of Addiction

Separation from a family where you feel that you are the one needed to hold it together is a very difficult task, which is why many adolescents from families who have been affected by alcoholism do not separate successfully (Steinglass, Robertson, 1983). Often they lack the skills to have close friends (O'Gorman, 1986). Many have been so involved in their families that they haven't devoted the necessary time to learning how to develop friendships. When they do begin to separate from their family, they may develop dependent relationships with their peers for they have not learned to do otherwise. In these relationships they will tend to become the caretaker, the responsible one (Black, 1979) and will form relationships with peers who need taking care of and who cannot accept responsibility for their own actions. Those who act out manifest their dependency in a different way (O'Gorman, Ross, 1986, Weiner, 1980). Both types are equally dependent.

. . . Compulsive Dependency

When Glynnis reached 16, it became apparent to Lisa that she was living through her daughter, just as her mother had lived through her. Yes, she enjoyed shopping with her, but she encouraged her to buy the skimpiest of bathing suits. She was as obsessed with her daughter's weight as she was with her own. She wanted to make sure that she only went out with the "right" boys, and she was careful to see that Glynnis didn't go steady as it was important to "play the field."

When Lisa, through her 12-step program, realized that this was not a healthy relationship for either of them, she withdrew. She decided to break with the family tradition of mothers living through their daughters. Glynnis felt abandoned, and found someone else to save, someone she could also rely on to tell her what to do. Her socializing from the time she was a pre-schooler had revolved around taking care of others. The two were synonymous to her. Having few social skills, and not having resolved her dependency needs, her dependency just switched its target.

The captain of the debate team became her new cause. He was a strong-willed, somewhat isolated young man. Glynnis was drawn to him. She felt that he needed her, and she began to take care of him. Her major decisions revolved around him. Lisa, aware that this was a continuation of Glynnis' relationship pattern with her, intervened. She made Glynnis aware that this was not a healthy relationship. Eventually, Glynnis began to see her mother's viewpoint. After many heart-rending discussions and increased demands by her boyfriend, she broke off the relationship. In the process she and her mother developed a healthier relationship which included more respect for each other's differences.

Glynnis had to face the fact that she was dependent on her mother, and didn't know how to make decisions for herself. Of course, she did know how to take care of her mother and now others.

When her mother detached, Glynnis panicked for now there was no one to tell her what to do and no one she could vicariously live through. By detaching her mother in essence had told her to live her own life, but hadn't prepared her to do this. Glynnis immediately found a substitute. When this didn't work, she needed an alternative and Overeaters Anonymous provided the best one. Through the OA program she learned to *rely on herself*. Glynnis began to make more of her own decisions.

. . . Acting Out

Acting-out behavior in adolescents is frequently misunderstood. While such behavior can have many roots, often it is a result of depression. This anger turned inward is masked by an outward sullenness and an "I don't care" attitude. Inwardly the adolescent may be hating himself and acting out as a way of getting punished (O'Gorman, Ross, 1986; Weiner 1980).

Acting-out adolescents deal with independence by stating that "it is no big deal." They are afraid but can't show it. They withdraw from their family overtly but manifest a high level of problems. The problems keep their family involved and close, albeit negatively. They can't leave home so they make sure that their parents do not trust them to leave. They can then safely rebel against their family, society, the world, knowing that if they keep acting up and they never need worry about being alone (Weiner, 1980).

Tim acted out by not only getting heavily into drugs but also by getting his girlfriend pregnant, as his mother Maggie relates: "To Tim, having a baby was no big deal. He was going to marry Connie and continue high school. He was in his junior year, as was Connie. They didn't believe in abortion and having their baby adopted and raised 'by strangers,' was out of the question.

" 'Who's going to care for the baby?' we asked? 'We thought you and Dad would. It will just be until we get out of school, just about a year and a half.' The crazy thing is we considered it. Gary and I figured that I could quit my job, and he could get a second job.

"It took Alicia, our 14-year-old, fade-into-the-woodwork child, to ask if we wanted to do this. Gary and I, both being adult children of alcoholics, knew we could do almost anything. The question was did we want to? This was much more difficult for us to answer. We had to stop being dependent and ask what was good for us to do and what would really be helpful to Tim. We decided that we didn't want to parent an infant again and that if we did it anyway, we would again be giving Tim a mixed message.

"When we told Tim, it was a major blow to him. Somehow he felt that we would always be there to bail him out. The best thing we ever did for him was to say 'no' and mean it. Tim began to have to grow up."

What To Do?
Let Go — But Be Structured

It is so difficult to let go. Your children are so precious to you. You know what pain is for you have experienced so much. Often to compensate you try to hold your children closer. This isn't good for you or for your children. How can you let go yet still give your children the love and support they need?

Respect the choices that your child makes. Remember that you can influence your child's choices but you can't control them.

Allow your adolescent to feel the real-life consequences for their actions. Don't over-protect.

Talk to your kids. Keep communication lines open, even if you have to initiate and you don't want to. Don't let your kids' resistance to talking to you stop you.

Don't be blind to emerging problems. If drug or alcohol usage is a problem, confront your child. If you feel their sexual behavior is irresponsible, speak to them.

Have clear rules with rewards and consequences. Don't accept excuses. Rather put your energy into refining rules than teaching your child to be a better excuse-maker.

Use your 12-step program. Remember it is a program for life.

Summary

Parenting teenagers for those recovering from the varied effects of addiction is tough. Sometimes, developmentally, there is not much difference between parents and children as both may be dealing with the issues of individuation and separation. To parent a teenager means that you have to grow, sometimes just to keep one step ahead of your child and not treat your teen as an outgrowth of yourself. The issues raised earlier bear repeating here. Consistency is important, as is talking to your adolescents. Most important is being the adult in the family. Your children need this, and you may even find it enjoyable. Remember, if you can't or won't parent your child, who will?

PART III
Living Through Addiction

Chapter 9

Parenting with an Alcoholic in the House

"I feel like I am drowning. I have three kids and a drunk for a husband. I never know what Dan is going to do next. He is great with the kids one day and a monster the next. No matter how hard I try I can't get him to stop drinking or using cocaine. I used to be an honest person, now I find myself lying to everyone about Dan's drinking and drug use. Sometimes I think it would be easier if I were a single parent. At least I wouldn't have to deal with all the chaos Dan causes when he is drunk.

"Last week we had a fight and it got very heated, and we said some very ugly things to one another. Later I found my five-year-old, Tony, hiding under his bed. Marcia, my eight-year-old, barely talks anymore and cries for no reason. Gina, the 14-year-old, has been getting in trouble in school. I'm under so much stress that at times I take it out on the kids unfairly. I am trying my best, but how can I be a good parent?

"Maybe Dan's right when he says, he wouldn't drink and use drugs so much if I was a better wife and mother. I just don't know what to think. I feel like I live in the middle of a hurricane and no matter what I do, my kids are doomed to be damaged by the both of us," says Janet, 32, and the wife of Dan, 36, an active alcoholic and cocaine user.

The Impact of Addiction

Living with or being married to an addicted person *is* like living in the eye of a hurricane. Everyone gets swept up in the whirl of addiction.

The spouse of the alcoholic often gets as involved in the obsession with drinking as the alcoholic but for different reasons. Husbands and wives of alcoholics spend a great deal of time and energy trying to control the alcoholic's behavior. The spouse of the alcoholic or drug abuser often gets as involved in the obsession with alcohol or drugs as the addicted person does but for different reasons and will get caught up in a maze of excuses and lies in the vain attempt to hide the severity of the addiction from the outside world and herself (Greenleaf, 1981). The spouse begins to accept more and more crazy behavior as normal for the family to keep herself from having to face the reality of the situation (Bepko, Krestan, 1985). Increasingly, the spouse of the alcoholic or addicted person begins to accept that it's OK for her family to live in a chronic state of tension and stress. In fact, stress and tension and unpredictability become normal for the family.

Janet is caught up in her own confusion and self-blame. She blames herself for her husband's drinking and drug use and feels like a failure as a parent. She has allowed herself to become over-involved in protecting her husband from the consequences of his drinking and drugging and in the process she has lost sight of what she needs to do to protect her children.

Parenting in an Active Alcoholic Home

Janet can be a good parent and she can limit the negative effects of Dan's alcoholism on her children. It will not be easy, but it can be accomplished. The single greatest problem alcoholic families face is that they let the alcoholic set the ground rules. The family mobilizes around the alcoholic's needs rather than the family's. The family responds to the alcoholic's moods and desires. If the alcoholic feels like going out to eat, everyone goes out even if dinner is already on the table. If the alcoholic is ill, everyone must be quiet. And always the family must protect the alcoholic, by denying the alcoholism and by pretending that all is well within the family. The children sacrifice themselves to the alcoholic for his arbitrary use, to be "loved" or victimized, while the sober spouse views herself as a victim of fate.

If the sober spouse is to parent with health, this contract to protect and cater to the alcoholic must be broken (Subby, 1983). The children must see that the family's needs are as important as the alcoholic's and that they have rights and privileges the same as their parents. The sober spouse must become a role model of self-assertion and independence and must give up the role of helpless victim. Living with an alcoholic need not define the family if the sober spouse is willing to take charge and set limits on the alcoholic's ability to affect the family.

This is no small order for someone in Janet's position. She will need to accept that she cannot take charge overnight. She will have to learn a whole new way of being in her family, and she will need to accept that she will not be able to do this alone. She will need to learn to reach out and ask for help so she can learn about alcoholism and drug addiction.

Some Basic Rules For Learning to Live With Addiction

Rule: Go to Al-Anon.

Al-Anon is a self-help program for people who care about or live with an alcoholic. Al-Anon is based on the principles of Alcoholics Anonymous. Al-Anon is a place you can go where you can meet people who have learned how to live successfully with an alcoholic. You will meet people who will help you learn how to detach from the alcoholic. You will learn about the disease of alcoholism. Most importantly, you will be able to get ongoing support from people who really understand what you are going through and how to cope with it. It is a safe haven, a place of hope and recovery.

Children learn how to deal with life by watching their parents. Al-Anon will teach you new ways to deal with life and the alcoholic so that you can become a role model of health and self-worth rather than a model of victimization and resentment. Al-Anon will help you to learn how to communicate positive messages to your children. Al-Anon will give you the help you need to give up the useless attempts to control the alcoholic's drinking and instead take control over your life.

Rule: Take charge of your family. Develop consistent patterns.

The first step in learning to live with addiction is not to let the addict control you or your family. Janet has let herself become an extension of her husband. Unfortunately, her husband has let himself become an extension of his alcoholism. His world centers around his need for alcohol. As long as that is true, Janet must not let her world center around him, or she through association shall become an accomplice in her husband's disease. She must learn how to love the man and refuse the behavior. She must learn the Al-Anon concept of detachment with love. The alternative is to remain merged to her husband in a constantly downward spiral, and having her children pulled down with her. She must learn how to support her children so they do not internalize negative messages about themselves. She must learn how to create calm in the face of the storm.

Be Consistent

Inconsistency is the hallmark of the alcoholic family. No one ever knows what to expect from the alcoholic. One night he may be warm and loving and extremely permissive and the next night he may be irritable and unduly restrictive with his children. Children in an alcoholic home never know consistent rules and therefore have trouble learning how to behave (Steinglass, Robertson, 1983). Planning is impossible if it is contingent on participation with the alcoholic. Mealtimes, birthdays, holidays or other events are always open to disaster if the alcoholic is needed for success.

Studies have shown that the disruption of family rituals like mealtimes, holidays and birthdays may have a direct impact on the transmission of alcoholism to the next generation (Wolin, Bennet, Noonan, 1979). Make sure you set down rules for your children that are consistent, even if your spouse tries to change them. Plan mealtimes, holidays, birthdays and other special events so that the alcoholic is not a central part of the event's success. Make sure that your children can go to the movies or the amusement park, even if he doesn't show up to take them with you. It will be more work for you to take this kind of responsibility but the payoff for you and your children will be worth it.

"I suddenly realized in Al-Anon that his alcoholism did not need to ruin *our* lives as well," Janet explains. "Once I got that idea, it became easier. We had dinner at the same time whether or not Dan was home. I didn't count on him to take the kids to ball games or on fun trips. We went on our own at agreed upon times, even if Dan had planned to be there and failed to show up. The kids were relieved and grateful.

"I realized this was the first time in their lives that they could begin to count on anything really taking place when it was supposed to. Dan began to realize that we were going to continue our lives with or without him. He learned that we loved him but we were not going to let his alcoholism control our ability to enjoy ourselves or plan our lives. The funny thing is even though he hasn't stopped drinking, he is drinking less around us because we do not accept his drunken behavior anymore. And you know, he shows up more frequently on time for dinner. He even shows up now and then to go out with us when he's supposed to.

"I think he got frightened because the first time he didn't show up to go out with us when we had planned, we left without him. The kids are feeling more normal all the time and given Dan's drinking, that's a miracle. My self-esteem has gone up, too. I no longer feel like a failure as a parent. I no longer take responsibility for Dan's problems. It feels good."

Rule: Validate your children's reality.

Children from alcoholic families are constantly forced to deny their reality. This is one of the most destructive aspects of growing up in an alcoholic family. Most children in alcoholic homes grow up learning to dismiss what they feel. Eventually they can no longer tell what they feel and become emotionally numb. You can help your children avoid this problem.

First Steps . . .
Admitting the Problem

The first step is to admit to yourself and to your children the fact that *there is a problem in your home* and that problem is alcoholism. It's not that the drinking parent doesn't love them, but that he just can't show it. Your chidren need to have their feelings validated by you. If you do this, you will teach them to face rather than deny their reality.

Janet explains how she learned to validate her children's feelings:

"It wasn't easy to learn to help the kids with their feelings about Dan's drinking and my enabling. The hardest part was learning to tolerate my own feelings of being a failure when the kids would express their feelings about our family. In the old days Gina, my oldest, and I would fight when she gave one of her, 'My dad is sick. When will you face that?' speeches. But as I learned myself about the effect my denial was having on the kids and became honest with them, we stopped fighting and became mutually supportive."

Trying to protect your child from the fact that one of their parents is an alcoholic and that the relationship between their father and mother is problematic is misguided. They know something is wrong, giving it a name helps them to be able to understand what is happening to their family and why. When you deny the problem, you isolate yourself from your children. When you admit the problem, you draw your children in closer to you and give them hope and a sense of security in the knowledge that at least one of their parents is healthy and unafraid.

Second Steps . . .
Educating Your Kids . . . Alateen

Children feel responsible for the problems in their families *unless* they are told otherwise (Ackerman, 1983). As we have seen it is a normal part of the developmental process for children to feel that they are the center of the universe and consequently responsible for the good and the bad things that happen to their friends, siblings and parents. It is especially important for you to explain that they are not responsible for a parent's alcoholism or for problems between their parents.

Children need a way to make sense of the world around them. As the sober parent it is important for you to learn how to explain the disease concept of alcoholism in language appropriate to their ages. You need to find ways to help them understand concepts like "drunk" and "blackout." Most children have no concept of what the drinking does to their parent. They don't understand that when Dad accuses them of lying about a conversation they know they had with him, he truly doesn't remember because he was in a blackout. Or that when Mom passes out, she is drunk, not dead. There are age-appropriate books available which you can use to educate your children. At the end of this book, we list books and materials which you might find useful in educating your children about alcoholism. There are also many contemporary movies which have alcoholism as a subject and could spark a discussion of alcoholism with your children.

Alateen is a self-help program for children of alcoholics. It is a place where your children can learn about alcoholism and get support for dealing with their alcoholic parents. They can meet other children like themselves and discover that they are not alone. The Alateen introduction from the book *Hope for Children of Alcoholics — Alateen* describes what Alateen is all about:

"Alateen, part of the Al-Anon Family Groups, is a fellowship of young people whose lives have been affected by alcoholism in a family member or close friend. We help each other by sharing our experience, strength and hope.

"We believe alcoholism is a family disease because it affects all the members emotionally and sometimes physically. Although we cannot change or control our parents, we can detach from their problems while continuing to love them.

"We do not discuss religion or become involved with any outside organizations. Our sole topic is the solution of our problems. We are always careful to protect each other's anonymity as well as that of the alcoholic.

"By applying the 12 Steps of A.A. to ourselves, we begin to grow mentally, emotionally and spiritually. We will always be grateful to Alateen for giving us a wonderful, healthy program to live by and enjoy."

Third Steps . . . Protect Your Kids

This may seem very basic and it is. Too often children of alcoholics report being angry at their sober parent because they did not stop the alcoholic parent from verbally or physically abusing them. All children deserve to be safe. It is one of their most primary needs. It is from safety that trust and self-assurance are built. If children are not taught that they are not supposed to be abused, they will learn to accept and even expect abuse and may become abusers themselves. A parent who protects her child is a parent who teaches her children that they are worthwhile and valuable people. She also breaks the cycle of abuse.

It is not easy standing up to a drunk. But if it frightens you, think of how terrified your children will be if you don't. Standing up doesn't mean fighting with the drunk. It means not allowing abuse to take place. It may mean leaving the house with your children when the alcoholic begins to get violent. It means making sure your alcoholic knows that you will not allow him to abuse you or your children and that you will go to the police if necessary to protect yourself and them.

Set Limits on the Alcoholic

Too often the sober parent does not go for outside help because of the fear she has that a public disclosure of her spouse's alcoholism will interfere with his ability to make a living. This protection of the alcoholic from consequences allows the alcoholic to continue drinking and gives your children the message that they must protect the alcoholic and not themselves (Cermak, 1985).

You can decide as a responsible parent to set limits on the alcoholic. This may take the form of refusing to let your children ride in a car with the alcoholic when he is drunk. It definitely includes getting help for yourself and your children even if the alcoholic doesn't want help. Setting limits on the alcoholic also means refusing to allow the alcoholic to get away with blaming you for his problems and to manipulate you or your children with false guilt.

Set Limits on Yourself

Having an alcoholic spouse leaves the sober spouse with a true sense of being abandoned. It is a natural reaction for the sober spouse to lean on her children to fill the void. But leaning on your children for your emotional supports puts an undue burden on them. You should recognize the need for your children to lean on *you* and for you to find adults with the appropriate ego strengths for you to lean on. Al-Anon will greatly help in this area.

Sometimes, as we have seen, sober spouses will put their children in caretaking roles in the family. This can take the form of being "mother's little helper" all the time to having the oldest or sometimes youngest child take care of the alcoholic when he is drunk because they are "affective" at handling him. This also is a mistake. The family is where the child learns how to behave as an adult. If the child learns that he or she is only valued as a caretaker, then the child is liable to become a compulsive caretaker as an adult (Wegscheider, 1981).

Being responsible for one of his parents also puts the child in a *parenting-the-parent* role. This is very destructive and *should be avoided*. It makes the child feel like a failure because he or she cannot control the alcoholic. It also makes the child feel shame for the parent and himself because the child knows even at a young age that parenting your parent is not right. You need to find other adults to help you with these tasks.

You need to protect your children from your urge to lean too heavily on them to help you with your spouse. It is this role of "little parent" that adult children of alcoholics most often report as the source of their bitterness with their parents (Woititz, 1983). You can avoid this with responsible parenting even if your spouse never sobers up.

Rule: Show your love.

Children of alcoholics need assurance that they are loved. Often they conclude that they are not loved by their parents or they would not drink, fight or threaten one an other, etc. When children believe they are not loved, they conclude they are not lovable and this impacts dramatically on their self-esteem and behavior (Gardner, 1976). The sober spouse is generally under incredible pressure carrying the load of the whole family on her shoulders. Often she will mistakenly assume the children know they are loved by her efforts to keep them dressed, fed and protected from harm.

Children are not that logical. They need tangible, constant affirmations telling them they are worthwhile and loved. This is especially true for children of alcoholics. They are insecure about being loved. They can't understand how a parent could choose alcohol over them. They assume that the alcoholic parent does not love them (Oliver-Diaz, 1984). They also assume the sober parent does not love them unless she tells them so and shows it. This is not always easy for either parent. The sober parent is often too emotionally exhausted to give much to the children. The alcoholic is usually feeling too guilty about his children to be affectionate and loving when he is sober, and often inappropriately displays affection when he is drunk.

It is absolutely essential for you to find ways to show your love. Hugs at night, reading stories to your children or just saying 'I love you' are wonderful and important ways to show your love. Children need to be touched with affection. When your child comes to you for attention but you are too tired to give it, explain why you can't give it. They will understand that you love them but you are tired. Let them know that the alcoholic loves them, too, but he is sick and incapable of showing his love consistently right now. You will find that you will be enriched and nourished by the love you share with your children.

Janet found that out with her children.

"It's been great," she says. "Since I've learned to be more conscious about spending quality intimate time with the kids, the whole house has changed. It seems calmer. I know I am. There are times I come home from the restaurant where I work as a waitress, and I'm exhausted. Invariably Tony will call me from his room and ask me to read him a story or give him a kiss good night. When I take the time and he crawls up on my lap and I spend time telling him how special he is to me and we hug, somehow I am renewed. I realize now when I feel my love for the children and show it, I get more strength."

Guidelines For Recovery

It will not be easy for you to change your parenting while living with an active alcoholic. It takes constant self-awareness for you to make meaningful changes. You will often fall back to old patterns but eventually step-by-step, day-by-day, you will begin to see changes in yourself and your children. The Al-Anon phamphlet, *How Can I Help My Children?* gives this checklist for parents which serves as a good guideline for parenting in a situation with active alcoholism. It may help you to identify areas you need to work on.

CHECKLIST FOR PARENTS (from *How Can I Help My Children?*)

Do I think of my children as people who have a right to my respect?

Do I make them feel stupid, inadequate or bad?

Do I humiliate them in front of others? Or do I correct them privately, allowing them to maintain their dignity?

Am I courteous to my children?

Do I habitually yell? Threaten? Nag?

How do I correct my childen? Do I attack their character? Call them names? Lose my self-control? Hit them? Make sarcastic remarks? Ridicule them?

Do I jump to conclusions, expecting the worst? Or do I give them a chance to tell their side?

Do I make a big issue over small things? Do I have the same reaction to small problems as I do to big ones?

Is 'NO!' my favorite word?

Am I consistent?

Do I use my children to try to control the alcoholic?

Do I resent it when my children seem to love the alcoholic more than they love me?

If my child resents me, can I understand why?

Am I more truthful with my children?

Do I try to set a good example? Or do I expect more self-control from my children than I do from myself?

Do I encourage my children to express their feelings and then help them to deal with them, or am I still so uncomfortable with my own feelings that I condemn them for theirs?

Do I set realistic standards for each child's age or do I ask too much or too little?

Do I make confidants of my children, burdening them with my troubles?

Do I let them be themselves?

Do I try to be tolerant when they make mistakes?

Do I praise them as much as I criticize? Do I praise them in front of others?

Do I really listen when my children speak? Do I try to understand the feelings behind what they are trying to say?

Do I let my children know they are important? How do I treat the things they make?

Do I apologize when I am wrong?

Do I set limits on behavior and enforce them?

Do I show my children affection and tell them I love them?

Summary

It is possible to set limits for the alcoholic while learning how to find ways to have your own needs met. This means you will need to separate yourself from the alcoholic's ability to manipulate you and your family to meet his needs. You must take charge of the family and create an atmosphere of consistency and security. Children need to be protected at all times from physical and verbal abuse. They also need to have their reality validated and need you to admit to the problems that exist in the family. Finally, children of alcoholics need reassurance that they are loved and that the alcoholic loves them but is not presently capable of showing it because he has a disease.

You can limit the negative effects of alcoholism on your children. You can parent effectively if you can learn to detach with love from the alcoholic and separate your family from dependency on his participation in family life. The best place for you to get the help you need to learn to live productively with an alcoholic is Al-Anon. Working the Al-Anon program will allow you to learn how to live for yourself. In Al-Anon you will find people like yourself who will be able to give you all the support you will need to help guide your family through the chaos and into health and happiness. You will find true friends who understand how you feel and what you need. You will learn how to reach out for help and break the silence about alcoholism. You will find a pathway to recovery for your family from the ravages of alcoholism. You will find out that you will never have to be alone again and that there is a hope for recovery!

Chapter 10

If YOU Are a Recovering Alcoholic Parent

"I don't know what's wrong with my family. You would think they would be grateful that I've stopped drinking but all they do is complain about how little time I spend with them. It would be different if I was out drinking but when I'm not home, I'm either working overtime or at an A.A. meeting. I'm trying to build a new life for them, but they're not the least bit grateful!" exclaims Jesse, age 38, one year sober and the father of 10-year-old Michael and 15-year-old Leann.

Parenting is a Learned Skill and Hard Work

There is an old saying in the 12-step programs, that if you take a drunken horse thief and he gets sober, you now have a sober horse thief. The same holds true for parenting. Getting sober does not guarantee that you will be any better at parenting than you were when you were drinking.

Jesse, like many recovering alcoholics, can't understand how his family could put demands on him when he is being so constructive. He doesn't realize that his wife and children have a need for him to be a husband and a father.

As a wise old man in Alcoholics Anonymous once said, "When you were drinking, your car was in reverse. Once you put the cork in the bottle, you shifted into neutral. But only through the conscious application of A.A. can you get your car into drive." Jesse's car may be in drive in reference to his sobriety, but it's still in neutral as far as his parenting is concerned. Like many recovering people, Jesse thinks that just staying sober should be enough for his family. He needs to learn that parenting, like sobriety, is a learned skill and hard work.

The Impact of Addiction

During years of active alcoholism you developed distorted beliefs about yourself and your family. False pride and self-will ran your life (Alcoholics Anonymous, 1976). You believed that it was safer to love alcohol or food than it was to love people. You believed that there were only two options in life, to be totally out of control or in total control. You believed that people were not to be trusted and that asking for help was a sign of weakness.

You learned to keep feelings a secret and to expect others to do the same. Your world as an addicted person was one composed of lying, using and manipulation. Everyone had to focus on you and your needs. During your active addiction you lived in a world of extremes. From one day to the next your children had no idea of what you might do. Most of the time your children were secondary to your addiction.For your children the first real test of your recovery is to see if you have really changed. And change for them means a lot more than just not drinking. For children of alcoholics, meaningful change means that you will be available to them to lend them support and guidance. It means that you will see them as a priority and make time to be with them; that you will see them for who they really are and not just as an extension of yourself. For children of alcoholics, *recovery means having a home that is loving and secure in which individual differences are respected.*

Some Basic Rules
For Making Meaningful Changes

It will not be easy for you to change. Change takes time and it comes in small quantities. In the early stages of recovery the family of the alcoholic does not trust that the alcoholic will stay sober and that any changes the alcoholic exhibits are for real. This lack of trust is often frustrating to the recovering alcoholic.

It will take practice and understanding on your part to accept the time it will take for your family to believe in you and heal the wounds of the past. You will need to be the best parent you can be *one day at a time*, letting go of expectations of rewards from your children and spouse. You will need to avoid the urge to make your family over in your new image.

In order to make meaningful changes, you have to learn new behaviors, new ways of acting and interacting. Just as it took *repetition and practice* to create a life of abstinence and recovery, it will take daily practice and self-examination to be a healthy parent. The rules that follow offer some guidelines for you to keep in mind as you begin to learn to replace old attitudes with new ones.

Rule: Remember that being a recovering alcoholic is only one of many roles you have and that spouse and parent are the most important roles to your family.

It is common for newly recovering alcoholics to either become workaholics in the attempt to recoup years of financial loss or become fanatics for A.A., talking or thinking about little else (Alcoholics Anonymous, 1976).

Like Jesse, many recovering alcoholics don't understand that they need to strike a balance between their roles as provider, recovering alcoholic and parent. Working the A.A. program becomes the recovering alcoholic's primary purpose. In their enthusiasm at finding a new way of life, alcoholics often forget that their 12-step program has to be incorporated into their lives if they are going to be more productive workers, lovers, sons, daughters, husbands, wives and parents. If real recovery is going to take place for the family, then the focus within the family must move from the alcoholic to the other members of the family.

Making Room for Family Members

Jesse was furious with his wife Sarah when she finally shouted at him, "If I hear one more time how the people in A.A. have changed your life, I'll scream. Nothing has changed around here. You still don't spend enough time with the kids and all you do is talk about yourself and your recovery! It was better when you drank. At least then you weren't self-righteous and sometimes when you were feeling guilty, you helped with the kids."

Jesse didn't realize that while A.A. had changed his life, not much had changed for his family. He needed to realize that he was focusing too much on himself and his needs and not enough on his wife and children. It wasn't easy for Jesse. Constantly talking about his alcoholism was creating deep resentment in his family. For his family to begin to see meaningful change in him, Jesse needs to be *more* of an example of the program of Alcoholics Anonymous and *less* of an A.A. proselytizer.

Learning the difference between practicing the program of A.A. and preaching is particularly difficult for parents in early recovery. But it can be done. You need to apply the program's principles to the way you deal with your children and spouse, not try to get *them* to apply the principles to their lives. That will follow naturally later, if you set a good example.

It is difficult for newcomers in the 12-step programs to learn a new way of life and find new ways to parent without feeling overwhelmed. In his first year of recovery, Jesse was simply overwhelmed by the demands of family and program. He could not conceive of a way to be a father to his children and deal with the stress of learning how to live a sober life. So he withdrew from his parenting role and left his wife with an unfair share of the responsibility for the children. Naturally, she became resentful and his children felt deserted and concluded that they had done something wrong. It was Jesse's sponsor who finally helped him find a way out of his predicament.

Jesse's sponsor told Jesse that he needed to learn how to work the A.A. program so that he could be a better parent. Jesse learned that saying the serenity prayer when his 10-year-old got out of hand was as useful to him as saying the serenity prayer when he wanted a drink. He learned how to apply the slogans and steps of the program to his every-day life as a parent. He learned the difference between taking a break from his children and deserting them. He also learned that he was going to be uncomfortable at times, and that, no matter what, he could not avoid his family.

Teaching Your Children About Alcoholism

Children often get confused when their recovering alcoholic parent attempts to explain alcoholism and the 12-step programs (Oliver-Diaz, 1984). As Jesse's daughter Leann observed earlier, recovering alcoholics tend to use esoteric self-help program language and concepts when trying to explain the disease concept of alcoholism. This often causes confusion and anxiety in the child.

Children need things explained in their own language, using concepts that make sense to them. Concepts like recovering from alcoholism "a day at a time" don't make sense to kids. Telling children that alcoholism is "cunning, baffling and fatal" raises their anxiety level. Telling children they are at risk for alcoholism may cause panic in them if it is not done with care and with age-appropriate language. Trying to explain too much too early in recovery might do more harm than good to your children.

Studies show that the natural reaction for a child whose parent has gone into remission from a serious illness is to *distance* themselves from any discussion of the illness once the parent is better (Rice, Ekdah, Miller 1971). This is a healthy thing for the child to do. It allows the child to experience a period of safety and security in the knowledge that the parent is better. Many recovering alcoholics in their enthusiasm from A.A. may overwhelm their children with information and concepts that they cannot understand or are not ready to hear. It is important to take time to assess what the effect of what you tell your children about your alcoholism will be, whether or not the child can make use of the information at this time, and what would be the most constructive way to tell your children what you feel they need to know.

You will need to educate your children about alcoholism. How you do it is almost more important than what you say. You need to give information in a way that will not increase anxiety and stress on children who are already stressed. You should describe things in a manner that assures them you are healthy and able to care for them. You need to emphasize that while you need help to stay better, you get that help in A.A. and you *no longer need them to take care of you.*

Remember, if you constantly focus on yourself as someone who is recovering from a disorder, your children, *especially* if they are young, will believe that you are not really better and continue in high states of anxiety waiting for you to relapse. Learn to talk about yourself in posi-positive terms. Don't describe yourself as "dysfunctional" or as a "sick alcoholic getting better." Your children will misinterpret your humility for honesty.

Learning Balance — Or, 'Why If You're Better, Are You Always Talking About How Sick You Are?'

Learning how to achieve balance in life is a major challenge for most recovering alcoholics. Alcoholics are people who love to live in ex-

extremes. In a family it is important for parents to share themselves and each other with their children. To accomplish this, recovering alcoholics have to find a balance between spending time with their family and their self-help program.

Louisa, a 32-year-old alcoholic and compulsive overeater, has been married for 14 years and has a 13-year-old daughter, Laurie, and an eight-year-old son, Jeff. She is two years sober and one year abstinent and for the first time in her life she has gained a measure of self-esteem and has a great deal of pride in her sobriety. Louisa cannot understand why Laurie gets angry when she calls herself a recovering alcoholic in front of Laurie's friends from school, or why Jeff is constantly asking her if she's all right. Louisa feels even more betrayed and hurt when her husband Ben argues with her about how much time she spends on the phone with A.A. friends.

One aspect of recovery is to give clear and healthy messages. For addicted parents this means expanding your horizons beyond your disease. "It's amazing," Louisa said during a counseling session. "My eight-year-old stopped me dead in my tracks last week. He asked me why if I was better, did I always talk about how sick I am. I realized I've been giving him the message that Mom isn't OK by my need to talk about my alcoholism in front of him all the time. Since I've become his Mom again instead of Louisa, the recovering alcoholic, he seems a lot happier and relaxed. I now go to as many A.A. meetings as I did before but most of them are lunch-hour meetings so I have more time with the kids at home at night, and I set time limits on my A.A. phone calls so I can spend more quality time with Ben. It has really made us closer and neither Ben or the kids have complained about A.A."

Rule: Own your own feelings and allow your children room to have theirs.

Feelings are a way of reaching into ourselves and out to others. They are the personal coins we use in transactions with others. We can count ourselves as autonomous people to the degree that we are in touch with our feelings and able to give them expression. In healthy families the adults help children identify what they are feeling and support the child's right to those feelings (Black, 1981). This is not easy for the person with an addictive disorder.

Addiction and Emotional Life

Feelings are threatening to the recovering alcoholic. Food and chemicals have been used to anesthetize your emotional life. The expression of any strong emotion is considered dangerous (Gravitz, Bowden,

1985). Because so many people with addictive disorders come from dysfunctional families, they have not learned to identify their own feelings and have learned to dismiss them. The recovering alcoholic is often on a parallel process of learning to express feelings as his or her child.

Often the alcoholic reacts negatively to the expression of feelings in his or her child because he or she does not feel adequate to respond. Alcoholics may have no history to draw on with their children in this arena. Too often the recovering alcoholic parent will respond to any sign of strong feelings in the child by attempting to put a lid on the child's emotional expression so that the parent's level of anxiety will be lowered.

Thus the child learns to dismiss or hide his own feelings or suffer the displeasure of his parents. This is a repeat of the cycle of denial that most addictive people went through as children. The cycle of denial or feeling breeds resentment and erodes the child's self-esteem. It also sets the stage for chemical or food abuse.

Learning to Survive the Feelings

Louisa's father was a compulsive gambler and womanizer, and her mother was a compulsive overeater. Louisa never had a chance as a child to express her feelings. If she tried to express any anger, her father would become rageful and beat her. She was not allowed to go through her "no" stage as a child. Whenever she began to express her sadness at her home life or disappointment with her father, her mother would dismiss her feelings by telling her things were not as bad as she felt they were, and then give her some sweets to eat to ease her upset. Obviously, this taught Louisa that sharing her feelings was not useful and that food is the proper substitute for parental nurturance. Louisa later had learned to substitute alcohol for food.

Louisa became alarmed when she found herself filling with rage whenever her child would cry or express anger. It frightened her to think that she might become violent with her child as her father had done with her. After examining her way of dealing with her child's emotional needs, she realized that she had also adopted her mother's minimizing approach to Laurie's expression of emotion. She realized that she had to become willing to deal with her hidden emotional life if she was ever going to learn how to help her child's emotional life to flower. Louisa worked on become willing to open up. She went through a difficult time, but she used her 12-step program to get the support she needed and was able to learn that she could survive her feelings. In therapy she was able to feel the pent-up rage she had toward her father and mother and find out that feeling never did not make her a bad person. She was able to experience how sad the child within her was and learned how to give emotionally to the eight-year-old Louisa so that she could give to her own eight-year-old son Jeff.

Coping With Stress

Becoming a feeling parent is especially stressful for the addictive parent. You must learn to *recognize* when you are under stress as a parent and take responsibility for developing coping strategies. Recovering alcoholics must learn to recognize when they need a break from their children and then find appropriate ways to reduce stress. Many recovering parents become overwhelmed and blame the child rather than taking responsibility to take care of themselves in an adult manner.

Louisa was having a hard time coping with Jeff's temper tantrums. She brought him to therapy because she felt her son was "endangering my sobriety." It was her reaction to her son's behavior, not her son, that was endangering her sobriety. Louisa hoped that therapy could fix Jeff so that Jeff would put no emotional demands on her. Louisa could not tolerate his emotional mood swings which were appropriate for a child his age.

With the help of her sponsor and a therapist Louisa learned ways to cope with the stress of dealing with her son's emotional needs. She learned that the slogans in the 12-step programs could help deal with her son's anger one day at a time just as it had helped her stay sober. She learned that her higher power would give her no more than she could handle in any given day. She learned that the stress of parenting could be managed if she worked her program.

Rule: Think before you act.

As the old Native American proverb goes: Walk a mile in your neighbor's moccasins, before you judge him. Try to put yourself in your child's place before you act out any spontaneous impulse. Ask yourself what it would feel like to be the recipient of the act you have in mind. This slowing down exercise will save you and your child many unnecessary upsets.

Impulse Control

The Oxford American Dictionary defines an impulse as "*a sudden inclination* to act without thought for the consequences." Most addicted people have problems with impulse control (Silber, 1974). They ate or drank on impulse. Often they married, took or left jobs on impulse. During the active addiction, a lack of impulse control affected their parenting.

Inconsistency is a chief problem for children of alcoholics. If your parent makes decisions for your family on impulse, you simply have no way from day to day to predict what your life will be like. If children one day can stay up and watch television until 2 a.m., and the next night have to go to bed at 9 p.m., they have no guidelines for setting their own behavioral expectations. They can't determine what's right or wrong behavior because the rules keep changing. The child also learns that consistency in their own behavior is not expected which breeds all kinds of difficulty for the child in school, where rules must be followed and respected.

For the recovering alcoholic impulse control is usually still a problem. Children from recovering alcoholic homes often report that one of the most frustrating aspects of recovery is that their parents still do outrageous, embarrassing things to them and that they can never predict what their parents will do next (Oliver-Diaz, 1984). As we have learned, security and predictability are cornerstones of a healthy childhood. If your child is still constantly on guard because you are so unpredictable or because they still fear that you will humiliate them by some thoughtless action, then you must take care to correct this aspect of your parenting.

It isn't just negative impulses that interfere with healthy parenting. Many people, especially in early recovery, are filled with all kinds of positive, loving feelings toward family members after years of not even being aware of their existence. Often, after years of being ignored by one's parent, the child becomes the focus of attention and frequent public displays of affection. Because the recovering alcoholic has such poor social judgment, especially in early recovery, these hugs, kisses and other displays of affection may happen unexpectedly to the children in embarrassing places.

Jesse's daughter Leann was especially upset with her Dad when he kissed her unexpectedly and told her how much he loved her in the stands at a high school football game in front of her friends. Jesse's intent was positive, but his impulse control was poor and he did not think before he acted. This behavior for Leann was just like Jesse's old drinking behavior in that he did not consider how *she* might be affected. It is important to screen all impulses before you act on them, even when they come from a loving place within you.

The recovering alcoholic often *confuses* impulses with actions and needs help in deciphering the difference between feeling, thinking and acting (Silber, 1974). All parents at times have negative impulses toward their children. But the recovering alcoholic will often judge himself harshly for harboring ill feeling toward a family member. This judgment will often lead to unnecessary guilt on the part of the parent for crimes never committed. As a recovering alcoholic parent, you need to learn that guilt is only appropriate for negative acts, not negative thoughts. You need to learn that it's OK to think anything as long as you screen your thoughts and impulses and only act on the ones that seem reasonable and helpful to your children. Give yourself credit for the level of impulse control you do exhibit, rather than punishing yourself for having the impulse.

Remember, most recovering alcoholics are themselves children of alcoholics and if you are an ACoA, you were probably parented in ways that helped breed the impulsiveness in your personality. You need to learn to accept how courageous you are in becoming willing to stay sober and challenge the past in order to make a better future for yourself and your family. Remember feelings are not actions, and feelings do not have to be acted out.

Compulsive Behavior

The flip side of impulsive behavior is compulsive behavior. The Oxford American Dictionary, defines compulsion as "an *irresistible urge.*" This is different from an impulse. A compulsion is repetitive. It is also restrictive and rigid. Compulsions are hard things to break, as any alcoholic knows. The compulsion to drink is the first major challenge that recovering alcoholics face and have to overcome.

But you are not out of the woods just because you have stopped drinking. There are many other compulsions that you will face as a recovering alcoholic which will need to be challenged. The clinical characteristics of compulsive behavior are:

- restricted ability to express warm and tender emotions
- perfectionism and preoccupation with rules, schedules, and order
- insistence that others submit to your will and lack of feelings elicited by this behavior
- excessive devotion to work and productivity to the exclusion of pleasure and the value of interpersonal relationships, and
- indecisiveness, fear of making a mistake (DSM-III, 1980).

It is easy to see how one or all of these characteristics can interfere with healthy parenting. If you enforce compulsive rituals, your family will feel locked in and hopeless. In a home filled with rigid rules, children get the message that only the rules count and people don't. The rigid application of rules is typical in families that breed alcoholism (Bepko, Krestan, 1985). The goal for the alcoholic family in sobriety is to learn how to live with consistent, but flexible, rules. In that way each member of your family will feel valued and secure. Then they will experience your house as a nest and not a prison.

Children need to be validated for who they are. They need to get the message that you love them as they are, not for who they might become. The compulsion to make your family over in your image will breed resentment in your children and continue the pattern of self-doubt and self-rejection so common in adult children of alcoholics. Learning to validate your children as they are and not giving in to your compulsion to make them over is a major step in becoming a healthy recovering parent.

Finally, you will need to learn that people are the most important *gifts* in life. Alcoholics are people who don't know how to reach out to other people.

Often the recovering alcoholic will hide in perfectionism or become a workaholic to avoid dealing with interpersonal relationships. As a parent it will be necessary for you to challenge your fear of interpersonal relationships and learn to be with your children, rather than avoid or judge them (or judge them by avoiding them). In this way you will learn to share in the joy you can have sharing life with your family, learning to live with love.

Becoming a Conscientious Parent

Examine what you are doing and why. Having an urge or feeling an impulse does not necessarily mean you have to follow through on those feelings. If you take the time to examine those urges and impulses you will find that many of them are best left not acted upon and that new and healthy ways for you to be a constructive parent will become apparent. Becoming a healthy parent calls for self-examination. Being conscious of the outcomes of your behavior allows you to make informed choices concerning your parenting. Becoming aware of your impulsivity and compulsivity allows you to be a conscientious parent.

Rule: Keep a child-centered versus a self-centered focus when talking to your children.

This is not going to be easy and it will take practice, but it is one of the major building blocks for healthy parenting. Always ask yourself when talking to your children, "Is this about me or them?" The recovering alcoholic is a self-centered person (Alcoholics Anonymous, 1976). This is not bad or good, it just is. Self-centered people tend to see the world as an extension of themselves.

For instance, when her daughter Laurie brought home straight As from school, Louisa's reaction was to tell her daughter how good that made her feel and how glad she was that her daughter was doing so well in school. She continued to tell her daughter that her good performance in school made her feel like she hadn't wasted her life because now Laurie would be able to do the things Louisa could have done if she hadn't become an alcoholic.

How would that sound if you were thirteen? Instead of making her daughter feel better, Louisa made her feel worse by making her feel responsible for her mother's emotional state. By telling Laurie how good she made her mother feel instead of reinforcing her daughter's own good feelings about her success in school, Louisa imposed a tremendous amount of responsibility on her daughter. She should be glad for Laurie's sake, not that her daughter must make up for her mother's mistakes. A child-centered response, such as, "I'm very happy and proud of you," would have been far more appropriate.

Being Child-Centered

Recovery for children begins when they can see that their needs have become primary to their parents and that they are *no longer responsible* for making their parents feel good about themselves. One of the primary ways that all children from addicted homes are abused is by the premature responsibility imposed upon them by their parents. If you think back to your own childhood, you will probably remember times when you felt imposed upon to make your parents feel better. Your substance abuse was a reaction at least in part to that childhood situation.

A child-centered family is one in which the children feel that they are *valued and respected.* This means that you see them as separate people. Louisa's compliment was all about herself. As a recovering alcoholic it is easy to fall into old patterns of self-centered behavior. In order to break the cycle of addiction, Louisa is going to have to learn to step out of herself and develop ways of speaking to her children that are child-centered and ego-enhancing. Make sure you give your children the message that while they are separate from you, they are still the most important people in your life.

Rule: Progress, not perfection, is the goal.

Perfectionism is a major problem for most people who have an addictive disorder. It is particularly destructive to healthy parenting. In simplest terms, perfectionism is the constant demand to meet excessive standards that are unattainable. The perfectionist always has a gnawing doubt that he or she is not good enough. Perfectionists believe that they can win love and acceptance through performance.

Belittling and chronic criticism are symptoms of perfectionism. The perfectionist minimizes all accomplishments. The perfectionist cannot enjoy any of his or her accomplishments because no matter how good it was, it could always have been better and the perfectionist will focus on the negative. All this failure in the face of constant striving causes depression, low self-esteem and stunted emotional growth. The need to undermine and downgrade everything and everyone creates intolerable stress on the perfectionist as well as family members.

Jim is a recovering alcoholic and former cocaine user with six years of sobriety. His plumbing business is successful, and he has become a respected community member. Jim's wife Mary an adult child of two alcoholics, is a nervous woman who is a recovering compulsive overeater. They have three children: Bobby, 14, Bridget, 15 and Andy, 8. Both Jim and Mary are perfectionists. Their house is immaculate. Mary is constantly cleaning and rearranging the house in order to get it "just right." Jim is the coach of his son Andy's little league team. Although his team has a winning season each year, Jim is confused by the low morale and lack of enthusiasm his players have for the game. When confronted by some of the players' parents on how much pressure Jim puts on the boys to be perfect, Jim's response is to give a lecture on the virtues of excellence and the power of pressure to build character. Andy recently became seriously depressed and began to talk about suicide, which frightened Jim and Mary into family therapy. In therapy they learned that Andy's depression stemmed from the insecurity and stress that their constant demand for perfection created. They learned that their inability to be satisfied with anything that Andy did resulted in Andy questioning his ability to do anything right. The resulting feelings of failure led him to think about suicide.

Accepting Limitations

The path to health as a parent is filled with many imperfections. If you approach the task of parenting with perfection as an ideal, you will surely fail. Admitting imperfection gives you the opportunity to learn and grow and allows your family the same room for growth. Everyone needs to make mistakes to learn, especially children. Those mistakes should be met with understanding. Goals need to be attainable for children. It is in the successful mastery of skills that children build self-esteem. If a child hears the message that he or she is not good enough, the child may grow up without the ability to enjoy accomplishments. The only way to avoid perfectionism in your parenting is to learn to be less perfectionistic with yourself. Freeing yourself from the bondage of self-criticism will allow you to find new joy in each day and lay the groundwork for healthy, self-affirming children.

Guidelines to Recovery

Making changes in old habits and learned behaviors is never easy. But if you apply the same willingness to learn and change that you bring to your 12-step program to the effort to improve your parenting, you will find the rewards more than worth the effort. Remember, teachability is the key to developing a new beginning for you and your family. Perfectionism is a major roadblock to growth. It breeds a defeatist attitude. As it says in the Big Book, "We are not saints. The point is that we are willing to grow along spiritual lines. The principles we have set down are guides to progress. We claim spiritual progress rather than spiritual perfection." Temper your parenting with the compassion for yourself and your family.

Summary

Parenting is affected by addiction. There are some basic pitfalls to look out for if you are a recovering alcoholic and a parent or parent-to-be. You need to be aware that your role as parent is as significant to your family as your role as recovering alcoholic is to you. The expression of feelings is threatening to persons with an addiction. They have often come from families in which the expression of feelings was forbidden or abused. As a parent with addiction, you need to recognize that this is your problem and not your child's. You need to work on being able to tolerate feelings in your family members.

Impulsive and compulsive behavior are both problems for recovering alcoholics. The recovering person needs to examine his or her behavior to assess its impact on children. The disease concept of alcoholism can be troublesome to children if not explained in the right way. Recovering alcoholics should be careful in their use of "inside A.A." terms in attempting to explain their disease and take care not to raise anxiety in their children or make them feel insecure. Progress, not perfection, is the goal. The healthy parent and family is the one that allows family members to make mistakes and learn from them. The healthy parent increases self-esteem in their children and offers a safe and secure environment. With self-awareness and discipline the parent recovering from an addiction can be a healthy parent.

Chapter 11

When to Seek Professional Help

"I kept working my program, but I still couldn't stop beating my kids. I was grateful when a fellow Al-Anon member suggested that I get professional help," says Joan, age 52, the adult child of an alcoholic, married to Pete, and an active alcoholic.

What is Professional Help?

Seeking professional help means going to a *degreed professional* for special assistance. A degreed professional has received special training in medicine or mental health, including psychology, social work or psychiatry and alcoholism. There are also professionals who work with learning disabilities.

These are just a few of the many specialities that exist. Having received special training, professionals are qualified to render specific services. Unless a person is trained and licensed, they cannot legally render a service, and they are not qualified to do so.

Choosing the Right Professional

It is often easier to choose a doctor than it is to find a mental health specialist, for medical problems usually give a clearer indication where the trouble lies. The basic difference between mental health professionals is the extent of their training and their ability to prescribe medicine. Only psychiatrists can prescribe medication. Social workers and psychologists cannot. Aside from this difference, they can all provide psychotherapy.

Make Sure They Know About Alcoholism

Mental health professionals may need to be questioned about their training in alcoholism, and their feelings about and experience with 12-step recovery programs. Too often alcoholism is ignored as a major contributing cause to presenting mental health problems.

Joan relates her experience: "I remember one psychiatrist I went to didn't understand that Pete's drinking was a problem. He encouraged me to go to the bars with Pete, saying that Pete was lonely.

"That was fine, but where do you find a babysitter at 8:30 on a Tuesday school night? Instead of going to bars and leaving my kids with sitters I didn't really know, I wish I had been going to Al-Anon earlier."

. . . Ask About All Medications

Just because someone has an M.D. does not mean he understands addiction. Joan tells a story about Pete going to a doctor for a back problem and receiving a muscle relaxant, and a renewable prescription for Valium. When Joan called the doctor and told him that Pete was alcoholic, he told her that none of the medicine was addicting.

Make Sure They Are Licensed

You need to be an *alert consumer*, and ask about the qualifications of the person giving you help. They should be licensed by the state to do what it is you are asking them to do.

Making sure that your professional has a license is important, not only to ensure that you will receive good service, but also to make sure that your insurance company will reimburse you for the services you receive.

Make Sure You Like Their Professional Approach

This is more of a concern in the mental health field where there are a number of approaches to dealing with specific problems. Some therapists will use more reflective psychotherapy, others will use strategic approaches, or behavioral modification. You may need to experience a specific approach to know if it is right for you. Remember, if you don't like it, you don't have to stay with that therapist. Find another one with whom you are more comfortable.

The Difference Between Professional Help and Self-Help

Self-help programs are peer-led groups. There is rotating leadership, and no designated leaders. The emphasis here is on everyone sharing their experiences. There is a minimum of group interaction, as the purpose of the group is to learn by hearing from one's peers, as opposed to learning by recreating in the group the same dynamics which are causing your problems in your life. By such sharings, isolation is decreased, and a new perspective is learned.

Professionals are trained *not* to share their personal experience. With a professional there is an emphasis on maintaining objectivity. That can be very helpful in having one reflect and own up to responsibility for one's thoughts and actions. Professionals are also trained to intervene in a problem. In professionally run groups, confrontations are encouraged and analyzed for the important personal information they contain.

Self-help programs have been found to work very well with those who are also involved in professional help. Recent studies found 45 percent of those in Al-Anon (Al-Anon Family Groups, 1984), and 31 percent of those in Alcoholic Anonymous (General Services Office, 1986) had or were seeking professional assistance.

Who Needs Professional Help?

Not everyone who has alcoholism or is the child or the spouse of an alcoholic, is sick (Anthony, 1974; Russel, Strasburger, Welte, Blume, 1983). Not everyone needs professional help. Many of the problems that result from alcoholism can be dealt with in 12-step recovery programs and through a development of one's spiritual side.

Spiritual problems may require consultation with professional clergy. They have the advantage of being widely available with predictable office hours. Many are open on Sunday.

There are some special problems that will need professional help of a different kind. Listed below are just some of these special problems for which a professional consultation is advised. If you or a family member has presently or in the past had any of the problems listed below, a professional consultation is a good idea.

1. Special Problems for Adults include:

A. Mental Health
- incest
- rape
- emotional problems, such as depression or anxiety
- uncontrollable temper
- marital conflicts

B. Health
- recurrent headaches
- recurrent stomach aches
- any recurrent body aches or pains

C. Addictive Diseases and Disorders
- alcoholism
- compulsive overeating
- gambling
- drug addiction

D. Spiritual
- need to understand God in your life
- need to reconnect with God in a more formal way
- need to be forgiven by God for one's actions
- need to experience God's love in your life

2. Special Problems for Children include:

A. Health
- fetal alcohol syndrome
- alcohol-related birth defects
- hyperactivity
- failure to thrive or grow
- frequent headaches or stomach aches
- any recurrent physical problem
- alcohol or drug dependence

B. Learning Disabilities
- difficulty in learning to read, which is placing your child two or more years behind their peers
- difficulty in mathematics, such as number rotation, which is placing your child approximately two years behind their peers
- difficulty in paying attention in school, being easily distracted or having a short attention span

C. *Mental Health*
- incest
- difficulty in managing their temper, resulting in peer problems or problems with authority figures
- stealing
- depression
- high anxiety
- undue shyness
- child abuse
- child neglect
- traumatic injuries

3. *Spiritual*
- need to understand God in your life
- need to reconnect with God in a more formal way
- need to be forgiven by God for one's actions
- need to experience God's love in your life
- need to feel secure

What Stops Someone from Seeking Professional Help?

The authors have found that after people come to the realization that they need to seek professional help, they may postpone making an appointment. They may have come to the conclusion that they need professional help because their 12-step program is not enough, or they may not yet be in a 12-step recovery program out of fear that they cannot face a group of peers. Some may even feel that they are failures, and beyond help.

Frequently *shame and guilt* interfere with persons seeking professional help. They tend to blame themselves and to feel hopeless. Depression may even become intensified as they realize that they are not getting better. In this way they become immobilized by their own sense of failure. This is unfortunate, for pain which could be alleviated is prolonged.

If you think that you need professional help, call a professional. They will evaluate you and give you their recommendation. The most you risk is someone validating your need for professional help. Validation of your feelings, while something that you may have little experience with, can feel great. Of course, you could also be told that you are just fine, and need only to either continue your 12-step recovery program or begin one.

Summary

Not everyone who has been affected by addiction needs professional help. But if you are concerned about the need for help, call a professional. Be good to yourself and arrange for a consultation. Either way, you win. Your feelings will be validated and you will be told you could use some professional help, or you'll be told you are just fine.

Chapter 12

A 12-step Approach to Parenting

"I remember when my father died. There was so much inside I couldn't express. I was lost in a sea of feeling. I really loved him deeply, even though until the day he died our life together was full of disappointment. At the end we got somewhat closer but we never made it past our fear of one another. I still wonder if he really loved me. I don't want my kids to grow up with those questions.

"I love my kids. If anything were to happen to them, I don't know what I would do. I am doing everything I can to see to it that my kids feel my love, that we do reach past our fear and that as their father I teach them a new way and give them a start in life I never had," says Jim, an adult child of an alcoholic and recovering alcoholic and father to Andy, Bobby and Bridget.

This chapter is about *showing your love*, sharing your love and paying the price that loving costs. No relationship you will ever have will be as intense as the relationship and bond you will have with your children. For all of us, but especially people affected by addiction, childhood was a time of bittersweet memories and unanswered questions. Like Jim, many adults raised in alcoholic homes grew up not knowing if their parents loved them. They grew up not knowing how to show love, unable to trust that love can exist without strings.

For many people affected by addiction, the first experience of love and concern without strings attached is in the 12-step program of Alcoholics Anonymous, Al-Anon, ACoA, Narcotics Anonymous, Gamblers Anonymous and Overeaters Anonymous. For many people recovering from an addiction, the 12-step programs have come to represent the first healthy family they've had.

"Most people can't understand why I say I'm a grateful alcoholic. They don't understand that Alcoholics Anonymous has given me a way of life more productive and satisfying than anything I experienced before. Before I came into A.A., I was lost. A.A. has given me a whole new way to look at the world. I have learned the value of honesty, compassion and fellowship. I have learned how to give and receive. Sarah feels the same way about Al-Anon. "One of the biggest bonuses of being in our 12-step programs is the effect they have had on our family. When we apply the principles of the program to our parenting, it works wonders," says Jesse, recovering alcoholic father of Mike, 10, and Leann, 15.

The 12-step Program and Parenting

The program of Alcoholics Anonymous has helped at least a million alcoholics to get sober and stay sober. Its simple guidelines for living have inspired a plethora of self-help programs, like Al-Anon, Overeaters Anonymous, Gamblers Anonymous, Narcotics Anonymous and Shoppers Anonymous, to name a few. All of these self-help programs are based on the 12 steps of A.A.

The 12 steps of A.A. are founded on the experience of the first hundred people who got sober in Alcoholics Anonymous. The 12 steps offer a combination of psychology, spirituality and good old common sense. They offer a program for living, incorporating elements of Eastern and Western spiritual philosophy in a simple and direct manner.

As Jesse pointed out, the 12 steps of A.A. can also be used to help you be a better parent and enrich the quality of your family's home life. You can learn to share your love, and to parent in a nurturing manner by applying the 12 steps.

The 12 Steps of A.A. — A Reinterpretation for Parenting

Step 1: *"We admitted we were powerless over alcohol — that our lives had become unmanageable."*

Admit powerlessness over your ability to protect your children from pain and become willing to surrender to your love and not your control.

The first step in recovery programs calls for a willingness to admit powerlessness and unmanageability. This admission lays the groundwork for all the following steps in A.A. The admission of powerlessness is also important for parents. *Parenting is really a struggle between fear and love.* The parent loves the child deeply and fears that harm will come to the child. This fear that one so loved can be hurt overwhelms the parent, and so parents begin to believe that they can control their fear by controlling the child and thereby protect the child from harm. This is of course as futile as an alcoholic trying to control his drinking or a spouse trying to control an alcoholic. It simply is not possible.

The attempt to manage one's fear for one's child through control is often destructive to the relationship between parent and child and breeds rebellion and anger in the child and bitterness in the parent. Attempting to control the child creates unmanageability in the home, forcing parent and child into oppositional roles (Schaefer, 1982).

The alternative is to accept that no parent can completely protect his or her child all the time. You as a parent need to accept that pain is not always a bad thing for your children to experience. Children will learn from pain. No amount of controlling will save your children from feeling some pain and hurt in their lives.

From this place of acceptance you as a parent can share your love with your children and teach them to protect themselves. This will bring you closer to your children, helping to create harmony in your home. Admitting that you are powerless over life and that it will only create unmanageability to try to control your children, sets the foundation for honest parenting.

Step 2: "Came to believe that a Power greater than ourselves could restore us to sanity."

Find hope in the belief that recovery is possible through faith and a willingness to work on yourself.

An old adage says that a man can live three weeks without food, and three days without water but he cannot live three seconds without *hope*. The second step brings hope to the family affected by alcoholism. Alcoholic families are filled with all kinds of learned insanity. The book, *Twelve Steps and Twelve Traditions*, published by Alcoholics Anonymous, defines sanity as "soundness of mind." Whether you are a recovering alcoholic, spouse of an alcoholic or adult child of an alcoholic, who can honestly claim soundness of mind in the face of all the damage done by compulsive drinking, controlling or eating? Any person from a dysfunctional family can identify behaviors which they call "insane." These behaviors directly affect your parenting.

With the help of the second step you can develop the *faith* to leave behind these behaviors and create a new vision for yourself and your children. Faith is the beginning of hope. If you believe that a power greater than yourself can work in your life, then many miracles are possible.

Step 3: "*Made a decision to turn our will and our lives over to the care of God, as we understood Him.*"

Reach out for help and acknowledge that you are not alone.

In the third step one learns to *ask* for help and let go of the need to have control over others. Asking for help is the lifeline for parents. Most people who come from alcoholic homes don't know how to ask for help, and are terrified to let go of their imagined control over their lives.

When you make a decision to turn your will and life over to the care of a Higher Power, you agree to do your share of the work but leave the worrying to someone else. Allowing a concept of a Higher Power to lead you in your parenting will open up new avenues of inner knowledge that you didn't think possible. When you turn your life over to a greater force than yourself, you also turn your children over. If you really let go of the need to control, you will find that your parenting will become inspired because you have stepped aside and let a force greater than yourself work in your life.

There are many moments in a parent's life when you think you are not going to make it through. When children run away, use drugs, get pregnant, come down with a serious illness — at these times you will need to draw on greater resources. The third step makes these resources available to you for the big and little events in your life as a parent. Drawing on these resources and attempting to find *good orderly direction* (another name for God) in your life, will give you the sense of peace one needs to face the challenges of parenting.

Step 4: "*Made a searching and fearless moral inventory of ourselves.*"

Take stock of yourself as a parent.

The fourth step lets you own reality. It enables you as a parent to *identify* your strengths and weaknesses. While this may be an uncomfortable process at first, the rewards you will reap will make the effort more than worth the struggle. You need to examine where you do well and where you have problems parenting and why. This should be done without prejudgment. You are simply taking stock of your parenting warehouse and seeing that you have enough of and what you lack.

This will include a review of your personality traits and how they may affect your children. It is common for parents to project aspects of themselves which they fear their children will act out onto their children (see Part II of this book), and thereby create a self-fulfilling prophecy. This is often acted out by recovering alcoholic parents who fear their children will do the things they did as children. Sometimes mothers who were promiscuous earlier in life will project sexual acting out on their daughters when in fact their daughters are far less sexually active. The fourth step is a time to take responsibility for the things you don't like about yourself as opposed to projecting them onto your children.

Working this step may also force you to face some upsetting facts about your parenting when you were actively drinking, overeating, etc. It is important that you face the reality of your children's homelife before you recovered so that you can avoid repeating past mistakes. This step is not for punishment. Rather its purpose is to give a clear picture of where you were, where you are and where you can go as an individual and as a parent. The Fourth Step is hard, but it opens the door to self-awareness and growth.

Step 5: "Admitted to God, to ourselves, and another human being the exact nature of our wrongs."

Learn to share your parenting issues with others without self-recrimination.

Guilt is the great divider. It separates you from your loved ones. If you repress the baggage of the past, you are doomed to continue to carry it with you. Step 5 can liberate you as a parent. Once you have taken an inventory, you can see the exact patterns of behavior that get you into trouble with your spouse and children. Maybe it's perfectionism or fear of intimacy that sets you apart from your family. Whatever it is, until you admit to yourself, God (as you understand Him) and another human being, you will unwillingly carry the burden of unnecessary guilt with you.

This is also the *sharing* step, the time when you need to talk with your spouse. Examine your parenting together. See what works for your family and what doesn't. By communicating, you can see what each of you can do to make your parenting more effective. With your spouse create a parenting team through an open and honest examination of your patterns of behavior as parents.

Step Five allows you the opportunity to develop real honesty with other people. By sharing the things you see that you would like to change about your parenting with friends and members of your self-help group, you will find that you are not nearly as bad a parent as you thought you were and that you have all kinds of opportunities for support and guidance when you need them. This step allows you to drop the pretense of perfect parenting and allows you to join the rest of the world of imperfect people parenting imperfect people.

Step 6: "Were entirely ready to have God remove all these defects of character."

Become ready to change by giving up the demand to be perfect.

Be ready to *change*. Change is scary; it is not easy to become ready to change. Whatever patterns of behavior we have nurtured in the past, we nurtured for a person. Usually we did things in a particular way as a defense, to protect ourselves or our self-esteem from being attacked or destroyed. Your defects are really the way the child in you *protects* itself from a hostile world. This is a poignant step. It asks you to parent the child within you in a new and different way. In order to become willing to change, you must face the child within and tell him or her that it is time to give up the old ways.

You will need to develop new ways to defend yourself when defense is necessary. You will need to find ways to protect your self-esteem that do not necessitate denying your feelings. Taking the sixth step means being ready to feel all your feelings as a parent and letting go of control as a way of defending against your feelings of vulnerability.

Step 7: "Humbly asked Him to remove our shortcomings."

Make conscious changes in your parenting by identifying specific strategies for healthy parenting.

Becoming ready and humbly asking for your parenting shortcomings to be removed sets the stage for your *spiritual growth* as a parent. One of the chief problems that beset many alcoholics or people who grew up in alcoholic families is self-righteousness. Step Seven is the great leveler.

In the seventh step you *ask* for help. This is not easy for people who have been affected by addiction. Generally speaking, one major symptom shared by compulsive people is an inability to ask for help. Asking for help with humility is even harder.

In this step you begin to make conscious changes of parenting techniques that are no longer effective. Your children will challenge these changes in you. You will need to let them know that you have discovered some ways to improve how you relate to one another and you are trying to apply them. Your children may even provoke you to get old responses out of you. This is natural. You will need to set firm limits on their testing, but this is a period they will need to go through as you begin to remove the shortcomings in your parenting, and as they adjust to your new style of parenting.

Step 8: "Made a list of all persons we had harmed, and became willing to make amends to them all."

Take responsibility for the effect your parenting has had on your children and learn self-forgiveness.

This is the step in which you as a parent learn to forgive yourself. It will not be an easy matter. In Step 8 you will need to be very specific about the ways you harmed your children in the past and become willing to take responsibility for the past.

Accepting the past as a fact and *without guilt* is the way to do this step. This will be difficult. The natural reaction for parents looking back over a disturbing past history of parenting is either to judge themselves harshly or to minimize the effect they had on their children. We have seen parents who have said that their addictive or dependent behavior had no effect on their children. This is not true. By the same token we have had parents come to see us who were sure they did irreparable damage to their children. This is, fortunately, not true either.

Accepting responsibility is *not* the same as being guilty. If you are the adult child of an alcoholic, it will be very easy for you to confuse guilt with responsibility. Taking responsibility for the past means that you accept the past for what it is, commit to changing those behaviors which were harmful and follow through on your commitment. But taking responsibility means being ready to be very specific in admitting the truth about the past.

One way to simplify this step is to make a list of *new parenting strategies* you can implement. Making a list of the new strategies will give you a way out of guilt and a way into responsible action. Deciding how you will change as you face what it is you need to change and who you need to change for, will release you from self-recrimination. You need to remember that no parent willfully hurts his child, and that most of what you do as a parent you learned from your parents and that no one is at fault. You need to recognize that you did the best you could at the time, but now it's time to do better.

Becoming a recovering parent is like becoming a recovering alcoholic. Recovering alcoholics are not guilty or ashamed of their alcoholism because they are working on themselves to get healthier. You can let go of the shame and guilt associated with your past history as a parent by becoming a recovering parent who, like a recovering alcoholic, accepts his problems and does something about them.

Step 9: "Made direct amends to such people whenever possible except when to do so would injure them or others."

Make amends to your children through healthy parenting without over compensating.

Making amends when the time is right will *support* your child in a special way. Many parents want to sit down and explain the past to their children as a way of making amends. This is not always advisable. In fact, any kind of open discussion of the past might best wait until your children are in their late teens or adults.

The best way to make amends to your children is by being a *better parent.* This is tricky for recovering alcoholics and ACoAs. The tendency for many who have had problems with parenting is to try to make up for lost time with their children. They attempt to become super parents to their kids as a means of assuaging their guilt over the past. This is not good for you or your children. Your children will sense the guilt in the motive behind your giving and not trust it. Or they may begin to manipulate you because of it, and then feel guilty for manipulating you. You do not have to be the best parent in town. You do need to commit yourself to being the best parent you can be. That is making amends.

Reading this book is making amends. It shows your *commitment* to learn more about helping your kids. Going to workshops or classes on parenting is making amends. Going to parent-teacher conferences is making amends. Being at the school play that your 6-year-old is in is making amends. Buying your child everything he or she asks for, or feeling like you must become a slave to your children's demands because you were a "bad" parent, is not making amends; that is doing penance.

Making amends as a parent should feel good to you. It means sharing your life and attention with your children. It means opening up your family to a healthy acceptance of each others' differences. It means giving permission for everyone to express feelings to one another. It means setting limits on your kids in a firm but loving manner. It means reaching inside yourself to heal the child in you that cries out for attention and love. It means becoming all that you were meant to be as a person, and as a parent.

Step 10: "Continued to take personal inventory and when we were wrong promptly admitted it."

Model being honest with yourself and your children and create acceptance in your family for imperfection.

This step is fundamental to creating a *healthy role* model for your children. It is the step in which you as a parent give up your goal to be perfect and give your children permission to make mistakes. It is the self-honesty step. Here, you teach your children by your example that they can be imperfect and still be loved by you. That is an important lesson for children of alcoholics!

Children from alcoholic homes often base their self-esteem on their performance. They learn from an early age not to make mistakes and if they make mistakes, not to admit them. This is very damaging to the developing ego. Children learn by example. Ultimately, most of what your children will take from you will come from them watching what you do, not following what you say. If you set healthy examples, your children will develop healthy ways of coping. Modeling daily self-honesty and self-acceptance will enable your children to learn to deal with life from a place in which their self-esteem is based, to paraphrase Dr. Martin Luther King, on the *"content of their character,"* and not how close to perfect they can get.

Step 11: "Sought, through prayer and meditation, to improve our conscious contact with God as we understood Him, praying only for knowledge of His will for us and the power to carry that out."

Learn to accept your limits in life and find your true spiritual path while allowing your children theirs.

Spirituality is an important part of parenting. Children need an understanding of life based on spiritual principles. Children need values to live by. These values and principles should come from their parents. You need to develop a way of seeing life in a cosmic context so you can give your children a way to see the world. Families without clear spiritual values are often families that are drifting with no anchor. Spirituality means many different things to different people. There is no special direction you should take, but you need to find an expression of spiritual life for your family.

Step Eleven is where you come to terms with the one essential painful truth about parenting, that in the end your children will be on their own, and that some *greater plan* exists for all of us. As Shakespeare said, we are all players in a grand play. Much of what happens around us we can't control. Letting go of what we can't control is the core of Step Eleven as it relates to parenting.

There is a prayer around A.A. that goes like this: "God, thank you for all you have given me, for all you have taken away, and thank you for all you have left me."

Many people who have grown up in alcoholic homes have a hard time understanding that prayer. It is only after you have worked the steps for a while that you will realize that your experiences as a child, even the very bad ones, have helped to make you who you are and that there is a lot of who you are that is good and positive and worth keeping. *Give thanks.*

By working Step Eleven, you are able to *"let go and let God."* You recognize your limitations to control your children or what may ultimately be their fate in life. You allow yourself to be guided by a greater consciousness. This surrender to a power greater than yourself allows you as a parent to do your best and let go of the results. When you work this step, you give your children up to a larger plan. You respect the fact that everyone must walk their own path and that you cannot control the choices your children will make in life.

You also open yourself up to recognize the path that you must walk. At times this may mean that your values clash with those around you. But in Step Eleven we learn to trust that spiritual voice inside that dictates the choices we must make in order to live life with integrity. We learn true acceptance as a parent. You no longer try to control your children, but try instead to lead through guidance and example. You are no longer able to be controlled by your children because you have let go of the need for their approval, as you become more separate and self-validating. You learn in this step to trust in a higher form of parenting that comes from understanding oneself in a spiritual context.

Step 12: "Having had a spiritual awakening as the result of these steps, we tried to carry this message to alcoholics, and to practice these principles in all our affairs."

Reach out to other parents in the spirit of giving and community.
There is another old saying in the 12-step programs, "You can't keep it unless you *give it away."* Sharing experience, strength and hope have been the cornerstone of these programs. It is why their members "keep coming back." It is in helping others that one reaches the highest levels of recovery. For the recovering parents, this means reaching out to other parents in need and lending a hand.

It may mean sponsoring a parent in your self-help group, by lending support and insight to others who are struggling in their recovery from alcoholism or compulsive dependency to become better parents. It may mean establishing a parent self-support group in your community. Every parent, not just those affected by addiction, needs support. Helping to organize a parent support group allows you to reach out to others who do not have the gift of the 12-step programs.

Step 12 for recovering parents certainly means *getting involved* in your children's schools. It may also mean getting involved with your community to establish or support recreation programs and substance abuse treatment and prevention programs. Carrying the message of responsible parenting means that you become an example of concern and healthy parenting and that you learn to give of yourself freely when appropriate.

If you work the 12-step programs to the best of your ability and face the challenges you encounter, you will become the parent you were meant to be, and the parent you yourself never had. You will learn how to lead your children in a loving way and give to the child within you all that he or she needs. You can have it all, but the effort must be *whole-hearted and sincere*. As the book *Alcoholics Anonymous* says, "rarely have we seen a person fail who has *thoroughly* followed our path."

Summary

It is important to remember that parenting is always a struggle between love and fear. It is important to remember that parents will try to control their children in an attempt to protect them from any painful experiences. It is important to remember that the best you can do as a parent is be an example and encourage your children to their fullest by being all that you can be. As a recovering parent you will need to take responsibility for learning about your children and developing new parenting strategies so that you may open new avenues of communication and self respect in your families.

Finally you need to follow the 12 Steps of Recovery, Revised for Parents:

Step 1: Admit powerlessness over your ability to protect your children from pain and becoming willing to surrender to your love and not you control.

Step 2: Find hope in the belief that recovery is possible through faith and a willingness to work on yourself.

Step 3: Reach out for help and acknowledge that you are not alone.

Step 4: Take stock in yourself as a parent.

Step 5: Learn to share your parenting issues with others without self-recrimination.

Step 6: Become ready to change by giving up the demand to be perfect.

Step 7: Make conscious changes in your parenting by identifying specific strategies for healthy parenting.

Step 8: Take responsibility for the effect your parenting has had on your children and learn self-forgiveness.

Step 9: Make amends to your children through healthy parenting without over compensating.

Step 10: Model being honest with yourself and your children and create acceptance in your family for imperfection.

Step 11: Learn to accept your limits in life and find your true spiritual path while allowing your children theirs.

Step 12: Reach out to other parents in the spirit of giving and community.

Appendix

Terms used

Recovery — The process of reorganizing one's life so that it is no longer centered on an addiction or compulsion, including alcohol and other drugs, gambling and other compulsions. For the adult child of the addicted or compulsive family or the spouse recovery means no longer being centered on the addict or how the addiction has affected you.

Alcoholism — A disease, generally genetically transmitted, in which one becomes physically and psychologically addicted to alcohol.

Familial Alcoholism — A pattern of family functioning in which family members are organized around and adapted to the addictive and/or compulsive behavior of one or more members of their family system. It is a pattern of family functioning which is predictable and painful, adheres to rigid rules of behavior that constrict the expression of feelings and is often replicated within future generations.

Compulsive Dependency — Is a type of *"learned helplessness"* that is unconsciously taught to children from birth. Here the child is systematically made dependent on something or someone beyond themselves. Individual needs are fulfilled through something or someone else and not directly. This leads to a lack of independent action, as the person or the activity on which the dependency is centered becomes the focus of the majority of the individual's emotional energy and time, in lieu of directly taking care of him or herself. Compulsive dependency results in not only increasing the likelihood that someone with the genetic predisposition to develop alcoholism or addiction, will begin to drink, or to use drugs, but also leads to other types of compulsive dependent behaviors such as those noted in adult children of alcoholics. These behaviors include the tendencies to:

— develop crippling dependent relationships,
— compulsively overeat,
— compulsively work,
— compulsively find relief from tension, but not joy in sex,
— compulsively gamble, and
— compulsively shop.

Compulsive Gambling — An addiction much like alcoholism, in which the need to bet is not able to be controlled.

Drug Addiction — Being dependent on the use of prescribed or illegal drugs, such as Valium, Librium, Cocaine, Marijuana or Heroin.

Eating Disorders — Compulsive and addictive behaviors which range from compulsive over-eating to self-starvation, anorexia, to binging and purging, bulimia.

REFERENCES AND
*SUGGESTED READING

Children

* Arnold, L. **Helping Parents Help Their Children,** New York: Brunner/Mazel, 1978.

Bandura, A.; Walters, R. **"Dependency in Child Development: A Study of Growth Processes",** Itasca, Illinois: Peacock Pub., 1971

Bandura, A.; Walters, R. H. **"Aggression."** In Stevenson, H. W. (Ed.) **Child Psychology,** (62nd Yearbook National Society for Studies in Education) Chicago: University Chicago Press, 1963, 364-415.

* Bower, T. G. R. **A Primer of Infant Development,** San Francisco: W.F. Freeman and Co., 1977.

* Chess, S.; Thomas, A.; Birch, H. **Your Child Is A Person: A Psychological Approach To Parenting Without Guilt,** New York: Penguin Books, 1976.

* Crowe, B. **Living With A Toddler,** Boston: George Allen and Unwin, 1980.

Erikson, E. H. **Childhood and Society,** New York: Norton and Co., 1963.

Gardner, R. **Psychotherapy With Children of Divorce,** New York: Aronson, Inc., 1976.

* Gardner, R. **The Boys and Girls Book About Step-Families,** New York: Bantam, 1982.

* Ginott, H. **Between Parent and Child,** New York: MacMillan, 1965.

Harter, S. **"Processes Underlying the Construction, Maintenance and Enhancement of the Self-Concept of Children"**, In Suls, J.; Greenwald, A. (Eds.) **Psychological Perspectives on the Self,** Vol. 3, Hillsdale, N.J.: Erlbaum, 1985, 132-181.

* Krementz, J. **How It Feels When A Parent Dies,** New York: Knopf, 1981.

McCall, R.B. **Infants,** Cambridge: Harvard University Press, 1979.

* Missildine, W. **Your Inner Child of the Past,** New York: Pocket Books, 1963.

Mussen, P. H.; Conger, J. J.; Kagan, J. **Child Development and Personality,** Third Edition, New York: Harper and Row, 1969.

Rice, E.; Ekdahl, M.; Miller, L. **Children of Mentally Ill Parents,** New York: Behavioral Pub., 1971.

Rosen, H. **The Development of Sociomoral Knowledge: A Cognitive Structural Approach,** New York: Columbia University Press, 1980.

* Schaefer, C. **How To Influence Children, A Complete Guide For Becoming A Better Parent,** New York: Van Nostrand Reinhold, Inc., 1982.

Schaeffer, H. R. **The Growth of Sociability,** Harmondsworth, England: Penguin Press, 1971.

Spitz, R.A.; Wolf, K.M. **"Anaclitic Depression: an Inquiry into the Genesis of Psychiatric Conditions in Early Childhood II".** In Freud, A. et al (Eds.), **Psychoanalytic Study of the Child,** Vol. II, New York: International Universities Press, 1946, 313-342.

* Youngs, B. **Stress In Children, How To Recognize, Avoid and Overcome It,** New York: Arbor House, 1985.

Adolescence

* Bell, R. **Changing Bodies, Changing Lives: A Book For Teens on Sex and Relationships,** New York: Random House, 1980.

Demone, H.; Wechsler, H. **"Changing Drinking Patterns of Adolescents Since 1960's".** In **Alcoholism Problems in Women**

and Children, Greenblatt, M.; Shuckit, M., (Eds.) New York: Grune and Stratton, 1976.

Finn, P.; O'Gorman, P. **Teaching About Alcohol,** Boston: Allyn and Bacon, 1981.

* Ginott, H. **Between Parent and Teenager,** New York: MacMillan, 1969.

Hill, J.P.; Lynch, M.E. **"The Intensification of Gender-Related Role Expectations During Early Adolescence".** In Brooks-Gunn, J.; Petersen, A.C., (Eds.) **Girls at Puberty,** New York: Plenum Press, 1983, 201-228.

* Kolodny, R.; Kolodny, N.; Bratter, T.; Deep, C. **How To Survive Your Adolescent's Adolescence,** Boston: Little Brown and Company, 1984.

Lewis, C.; Lewis, M.A. **"Peer Pressure and Risk-Taking Behaviors in Children",** *American Journal of Public Health,* Vol. 74, No. 6, 1984, 580-584.

Morrow, W.; Robert, W. **"Family Relations of Bright High Achieving and Underachieving High School Boys",** *Child Development,* Vol. 32, No. 50/10, 1961.

O'Gorman, P.; Lacks, H., **Aspects of Youthful Drinking,** New York: The National Council on Alcoholism, 1979.

Simmons, R.G.; Rosenberg, F. **"Sex, Sex Roles, and Self-Image",** *Journal of Youth and Adolescence,* Vol. 4, 1975, 229-258.

Weiner, I.B. **Psychopathology in Adolescence,** New York: Wiley, 1980.

Children of Alcoholics

* Ackerman, R.J., **Children of Alcoholics: A Guidebook For Educators, Therapists and Parents,** (2nd ed), Holmes Beach, Florida: Learning Publications, 1983.

* Al-Anon Family Groups, **How Can I Help My Children,** New York: Al-Anon Family Groups, 1979.

* Alateen: **Hope For Children of Alcoholics,** New York: Al-Anon Family Groups, 1980.

Anthony, J. E. **"The Syndrome of the Psychologically Invulner-**

able Child" In Anthony, J. E., Koupernick, C. (Eds.) **The Child in the Family; Yearbook of the International Association for Child Psychiatry and Allied Professionals,** Vol. 3, New York: John Wiley and Sons, 1974, 529-544.

Black, C. **"Children of Alcoholics",** Alcohol Health and Research World, Vol. 4, No. 1, 1979, 23-27.

* Black, C. **It Will Never Happen To Me,** Denver: Medical Administration Co., 1981.

* Black, C. **Repeat After Me: Workbook for Adult Children,** Denver: Medical Administration Co., 1985.

Black, C.; Bucky, S.; Wilder-Padilla, S. **"The Interpersonal and Emotional Consequences of Being an Adult Child of an Alcoholic",** The International Journal of the Addictions, Vol. 21, No. 2, 1986, 213-231.

Bepko, C.; Krestan, J. **The Responsibility Trap,** New York: The Free Press, 1985.

* Cermak, T. **A Primer on Adult Children of Alcoholics,** Pompano Beach, Fl.: Health Communications, 1985.

Friel, J.; Subby, R.; Friel, L. **Co-dependency and the Search for Identity,** Pompano Beach, Fl.: Health Communications, Inc., 1984.

Goodwin, D.; Schulsinger, F.; Hermansen, L.; Guze, S.; Winokur, G. **"Alcoholic Problems in Adoptees Raised Apart from Alcoholic Biologic Parents",** Archives of General Psychiatry, Vol. 28, 1973, 238-243.

* Gravitz H.L.; Bowden, J.D. **Guide To Recovery: A Book For Adult Children of Alcoholics,** Holmes Beach, Fl.: Learning Publications, 1985.

* Greenleaf, J. **Co-Alcoholic, Para-Alcoholics,** Los Angeles: Jael Greenleaf, 1981.

James, J. E.; Goldman, M. **"Behavior Trends of Wives of Alcoholics",** Quarterly Journal of Studies on Alcohol, Vol. 32, 1971, 373-381.

* Kritsberg, W. **The Adult Children of Alcoholics Syndrome: From Discovery to Recovery,** Pompano Beach, Fl.: Health Communications, 1986.

Nardi, P. M. **"Children of Alcoholics: A Role — Theoretical**

Perspective", *Journal of Social Psychology*, Vol. 115, 1981, 237-245.

Nici, J. **"Wives of Alcoholics as Repeaters"**, *Journal of Studies on Alcohol*, Vol. 40, No. 7, 1979, 677-682.

O'Gorman, P. **"Alcoholism, the Family Disease"**, *Urban Health, Journal of Health Care in the Cities:* Special Edition, Public Health, October, 1974.

O'Gorman, P. **"Self-Concept, Locus of Control, Perception of Father in Adolescents in Severe Problem Drinking, Recovering Alcoholic and Non-alcoholic Homes."** Unpublished doctoral dissertation, Fordham University, 1975.

O'Gorman, P. **"Alateen — Why Refer? A Psychologists' Viewpoint"**, **Al-Anon Faces Alcoholism,** 2nd Edition, New York: Al-Anon Family Group Headquarters, Inc., 1984, 55-62.

O'Gorman, P.; Ross, R. **"Children of Alcoholics in the Juvenile Justice System"**, In Ackerman, R. (Ed.) **Growing In The Shadow: Children of Alcoholics,** Pompano Beach, Fl.: Health Communications, 1986.

Oliver-Diaz, P.; Slotwinski, J., **"Helping Children To Help Themselves"**, *Focus on Family and Chemical Dependency*, Vol. 7, No. 2, Mar./Apr. 1984, 36-37.

Oliver-Diaz, P. **"Self-Help Groups Through Children's Eyes"**, **Focus on Family and Chemical Dependency,** Vol. 8, No. 2, Mar./Apr. 1985, 28-29, 38.

Oliver-Diaz, P. **"Self-Help Groups Through Children's Eyes"**, *Focus on Family and Chemical Dependency*, Vol. 8, No. 2, Mar./Apr. 1985, 28-29, 38.

Oliver-Diaz, P. **"Teenage Co-dependents: The Chemical is Not the Issue"**, *Focus on Family and Chemical Dependency*, Vol. 8, No. 1, Jan./Feb. 1985, 17-19.

Russel. M.; Strasburger, E. L.; Welte, J. W.; Blume, S. B. **"Factors Associated with Coping in Successful Adult Children of Alcoholics"**, **Alcoholism: Clinical and Experimental Research,** Vol. 7, No. 120 (Abstract), 1983.

* Wegscheider, S. **Another Chance: Hope and Health for the Alcoholic Family,** Palo Alto, Calif.: Science and Behavior Books, 1981.

Wilson, C.; Oxford, J. **"Children of Alcoholics: Report of a Preliminary Study and Comments on the Literature,"** *Journal of Studies on Alcohol*, Vol. 39, No. 1, 1978, 121-142.

* Whitfield, C. **Healing the Child Within,** Pompano Beach, FL: Health Communications, Inc., 1987.

* Woititz, J. G. **The Struggle for Intimacy,** Pompano Beach, Fl.: Health Communications, Inc., 1985.

* Woititz, J. G. **Adult Children of Alcoholics,** Pompano Beach, Fl.: Health Communications, Inc., 1983.

Eating Disorders

* Hollis J. **Fat is a Family Affair,** Minneapolis, Minn.: Hazelden, 1985.

Hood, J; Moore, T.E.; Garner, D.M. **"Locus of Control as a Measure of Ineffectiveness in Anorexia Nervosa,"** *Journal of Consulting and Clinical Psychology*, Vol. 50, 1982, 3-13.

Schwartz, R.C.; Barrett, M.J.; Saba, G. **"Family Therapy for Bulimia".** In Garner, D. M.; Garfinkel, P. E. (Eds.) **Handbook for Psychotherapy for Anorexia Nervosa and Bulimia,** New York: Guilford, 1985, 280-307.

Selvini-Palazzoli, M. **Self-Starvation: From Individuation To Family Therapy in the Treatment of Anorexia Nervosa.** New York: Aronson, 1978.

Steele, C.I. **"Weight Loss Among Teenage Girls: An Adolescent Crisis",** *Adolescence*, Vol. 15, 1980, 823-829.

Striegel-Moore, L.; Silberstein, L.; Rodin, J. **"Toward an Understanding of Risk Factors for Bulimia",** *American Psychologist*, Vol. 41, No. 3, 1986, 246-263.

Alcoholism

Al-Anon Family Groups, **An Al-Anon/Alateen Member Survey,** No. 292-1-84, New York: Al-Anon Family Groups, 1984.

* Al-Anon Family Groups, **One Day at a Time in Al-Anon,** New York: Al-Anon Family Groups, 1973.

* Alcoholics Anonymous World Service, **Alcoholics Anonymous,** New York: Alcoholics Anonymous World Service, 1976.

* Alcoholics Anonymous World Service, **Twelve Steps and Twelve Traditions,** New York: Alcoholics Anonymous World Service, 1981.

Bowen, M. **"A Family Systems Approach to Alcoholism",** *Addiction,* A Quarterly Publication of the Addiction Research Foundation, Toronto, Canada, Summer, Vol. 21, No. 2., 1974.

General Services Office, Alcoholics Anonymous, personal communication, 1986.

Jackson, J. K. **"The Adjustment of the Family to the Crises of Alcoholism",** *Quarterly Journal of Studies on Alcohol,* Vol. 15, 1954, 562-586.

* Milam, J.; Ketcham, K. **Under the Influence,** Seattle: Madrona Pub., 1981.

Moos, R.; Moos, B. **"The Process of Recovery from Alcoholism: Comparing Functioning in Families of Alcoholics and Matched Control Families",** *Journal of Studies on Alcohol,* Vol. 45, March, 1984.

O'Gorman, P. **"Alcoholism, the Family Disease",** **Urban Health,** *Journal of Health Care in the Cities;* Special Edition, Public Health, October 1974.

Russell, M. **"The Epidemiology of Alcohol-Related Birth Defects"** In Abel, E.L., (Ed.) **Fetal Alcohol Syndrome, Vol. II: Human Studies,** Boca Raton, Fl: CRC Press, Inc., 1982, 89-126.

Silber, A. **"Rationale for the Technique of Psychotherapy with Alcoholics",** *International Journal of Psychoanalytic Psychotherapy,* 1974, 28-47.

Steinglass, P. **"A Life History Model of the Alcoholic Family",** Vol. 19, No. 3, 1980, 211-226.

Steinglass, P.; Robertson, A. **"The Alcoholic Family",** In Kissin, B.; Begleiter, H. (Eds), **The Biology of Alcoholism,** Vol. 6: **The Pathogenesis of Alcoholism, Psychosocial Factors,** New York: Plenum Press, 1983, 243-307.

Strauss, R. **"Conceptualizing Alcoholism and Alcohol Problems".** In O'Gorman, P.; Smith I.; and Stringfield, S. (Eds.) **Defining Adolescent Alcohol Use, Implications Toward a Defini-**

tion of Adolescent Alcoholism, New York: National Council on Alcoholism, 1976, 106-107.

Wallace J. Alcoholism: New Light on the Disease. Chapel Hill: Lexis Press, 1985.

Whitfield, C. Alcoholism and Spirituality, Baltimore: The Resource Group, 1985.

Wolin, S.J.; Bennet, L.A.; Noonan, D. L. "Family Rituals and the Recurrence of Alcoholism over Generations", American Journal of Psychiatry, Vol. 136, 1979, 589-593.

Gambling

Blaszczynski, A. "Brain Chemistry and the Gambler's High", Psychology Today, May 1985.

Blaszczynski, A. "A Winning Bet: Treatment for Compulsive Gambling", Psychology Today, Dec. 1985.

Holden, C. "Against All Odds", Psychology Today, Dec. 1985.

Family Therapy/Couple Therapy

Campbell, S. Beyond the Power Struggle, San Luis Obispo: Impact Publishers, 1984.

Papp, P. The Process of Change. New York: The Guilford Press, 1983.

Endorsements

"In Breaking the Cycle, O'Gorman and Diaz present a sensitive and timely guide for parents affected by alcoholism. I will enthusiastically recommend this book to both my recovering patients and to treatment professionals."

— **John W. Thomas, M.D.**
Internal Medicine/Substance Abuse

"Future generations will owe much to people like Pat O'Gorman and Philip Oliver-Diaz. They are members of a first generation of Adult Children of Alcoholics who were courageous enough to break out of the endless cycle of dysfunction that occurs in alcoholic families and is unconsciously handed down to subsequent generations. This book is their gift to millions of others. It teaches adults who grew up in alcoholic homes how to break the cycle, how to prevent it from being handed down and best of all, how to enjoy one of life's most precious gifts — our own children."

— **Sue Rusche**
Director
Families in Action
and syndicated newspaper columnist
on drug and alcohol abuse

"Based on relevant developmentally accurate data and written in a concise, clear, understandable manner, Breaking the Cycle of Addiction breaks ground and builds a solid foundation upon which all members of alcoholic families can build a new non-addictive future."

— Zvi Klopott, M.D.
Child Psychiatrist

"Breaking the Cycle of Addiction promises to be a significant, realistic and generous contribution to the health of our children.

In working with guilt-ridden and often compulsive addictive parents, pediatricians have long seen the need for helping those parents develop better parenting skills and for treating addiction in the family with compassion.

This book answers both needs remarkably well."

— Donald Ian Macdonald, M.D.
Administrator
Alcohol, Drug Abuse, and Mental Health
Administration (ADAMHA)

"O'Gorman and Diaz have a unique way of addressing a dark and complex subject and bringing it to a level that is both humanistic and instructional. Once a parent digests the many levels of information presented in this book, they will surely have the ammunition to begin to break the cycle."

— Susan K. Newman
Executive Director
Scott Newman Foundation